FLAMED BY THE SPIRIT

FLAMED BY THE SPIRIT

Biblical Definitions of
the Holy Spirit
A Brethren Perspective

Dale W. Brown

The Brethren Press
Elgin, Illinois

Copyright © 1978, The Brethren Press
Printed in the United States of America
All rights reserved.
Cover design: Wilbur Brumbaugh/Ken Stanley

Library of Congress Cataloging in Publication Data

Brown, Dale W., 1926-
    Flamed by the Spirit.

    Includes bibliographical references.
    1. Holy Spirit—Biblical teaching. 2. Gifts,
Spiritual—Biblical teaching. 3. Pentecostalism.
I. Title.
BS680.H56B76   231'.3   78-8212
ISBN O-87178-277-4

CONTENTS

FLAMED BY THE SPIRIT

Are we truly in the Age of the Spirit?

We do know there are many things blowing in the wind . . .
   a new pentecostalism in our midst
      freer expressions of feeling
         appropriation of what the blacks call soul
            the frenzy of the sound of rock
               yearnings toward mysticism, spiritualism, yoga, and Zen
                  disciplines
               the enthusiasm and warmth of Jesus people.

Such stirrings often judge our neglect of deeper dimensions of human existence and of the gospel.

For this reason we should live in fresh expectancies of being *flamed by the spirit.*

As Christians we need to turn anew to biblical expressions which point to the third person of the trinity. . . .

If we daily die to the old and expect new life and vitality, we can be *flamed by the spirit.* Healings, miracles, prophecies, and other biblical gifts *can* be expected today.

If we test the spirits by the man for others who died on the cross we can be *flamed by the spirit.*

If we truly know the church as the community of the Spirit, we can be *flamed by the spirit.*

If we look for the Spirit's coming in those things which make for peace, for justice, for righteousness, we can be *flamed by the spirit.*

Dale W. Brown
Annual Conference, 1972

PREFACE

In response to the invitation to lead the Bible hours for the National Youth Conference at Estes Park, Colorado, 1962, I suggested four passages dealing with the Holy Spirit. Some staff-planners were dismayed. They were certain that youth would be turned off by the topic. Because leaders had been appointed and the presentations plus the group discussions were to be such a major part of the program, they feared for the success of the entire conference. Only the greater degree of openness on the part of some youth on the committee combined with my stubbornness to save the suggestion. There was surprise that the youth became as involved as they did as the doctrine of the Spirit came alive during that conference.

This occurred the same summer in which I received my doctorate upon the completion of a dissertation on a Spirit-related topic, the problem of subjectivism in Pietism. My research had attempted to deal with many issues of Christian experience which were a part of the milieu of the early Brethren. My adviser thought it should be published. We tried but to no avail. I doubt that even the presence of some youth on the editorial staff of the publisher would have made a difference.

Sixteen years later, with another National Youth Conference to be held in the same spot in the Rockies, I have been asked to speak again. This time the topic, power, has been assigned. Even more indicative of the changed mood, however, is that in this same year a revision of my dissertation, *Understanding Pietism* (Eerdmans, 1978), is being published, as well as this board-and-staff-initiated study, *Flamed by the Spirit*. I write appreciatively, because this small book reflects the development of some of the seeds sown at Estes in 1962. Likewise, I think it appropriate to dedicate both books to Floyd E. Mallott, who first engendered my interest in experiential theology. I hope the book reflects indebtedness to charismatics who have helped the doctrine come alive in new ways for my life and thought.

Because of the current interest, several excellent books have appeared recently which deal biblically and theologically with the doctrine of the Holy Spirit. In reading these in preparation for this assignment, I began to feel that there might not be a need for another. The only excuse for this treatment is to look at Spirit phenomena through Brethren eyes and digest some of the best of present scholarship for consumption by Brethren and similar groups. It is not that Brethren can add many unique insights. But our communal theology and experience means that we bring a focus which may lead to a greater clarity about biblical definitions, because of the corporate orientation of the sacred writers themselves.

Anyone who currently writes needs to struggle with the issue of sexist language. My own position is one of desiring not to offend and to become more inclusive of all as I write. For this reason, I desire to be corrected by editors and others when I am not. At the same time, it is difficult for me to change words in quoting those who have lived before, because I want to be as true as possible to what they believed and represented as they wrote. My thanks to Rick Gardner and others on the staff for helping me through this problem and others.

Likewise, I want to mention Wilbur Brumbaugh, who originally worked with me in planning this manuscript. In our shared leadership responsibilities for the 1972 Annual Conference, it was his creativity which provided the artistic support for the theme, "Flamed by the Spirit," and which has been appropriated for the title of this book.

Finally, I need to thank Berea College in Kentucky for freeing me from my duties as visiting professor during January, 1978, which time I utilized to put this book in final form.

Dale W. Brown

Chapter 1

THE SPIRIT GIVES LIFE

"For the letter killeth, but the spirit giveth life"
(2 Corinthians 3:6 KJV)

Spirit in the Bible

In the earliest biblical traditions, spirit is the life-breath received directly from God. Through God's inbreathing, "inspiration," we become living persons. Biblical words for spirit such as *ruach* in Hebrew and *pneuma* in Greek can also mean wind or breath. *Ruach* suggests that *the Spirit* is God in action. The Spirit of God is an invading force. God's *ruach* can infuse new life into dry bones (Ezek. 37). Biblical metaphors such as "mighty wind" and "tongues of fire" point to the availability of power when we receive the Holy Spirit (Acts 1:8). It may be right to expect God to speak in a gentle whisper, but the Bible suggests the possibility of a roaring wind. The Spirit is the personal, moral, active power of God.

For the most part the Bible does not divide a person into parts. We are acquainted with the body-soul division which defines the body part of us as earthy and the soul part as immortal. The creation accounts do not speak of an imprisoned soul so much as a single entity, an animated body, a living person. Neither do the biblical writers delineate neatly any of the three-part divisions, such as body, soul, and spirit—or body, mind, and spirit. Rather than the spirit being a part of us, the spirit is that quality and power which give life to our entire being. To be fleshly is often interpreted to mean that we cater to our bodily desires. In the Pauline sense, however, to be fleshly is to center our lives in such a way that our emotions, minds *and* desires are out of proper relationship with God and others. To be spiritual, on the other hand, is to be so filled by the Spirit that our total being is oriented toward a right relationship with God and our fellow creatures. To live and walk in the Spirit is to respond to God's gift of life by loving with all heart, soul, and mind (Matt. 22:37).

Starting from the assumption that all life is a gift from God, it was natural that the biblical writers likewise regarded special qualities, abilities, and knowledge as gifts from the Lord. The first special gift of the Spirit in the Bible may have been the endowing of Joseph with the gift of interpreting dreams for the common good. Similar divine impulses were recorded to have manifested themselves in persons in the form of prophecy, special wisdom, healings, ecstatic behavior, leadership potentialities, and moral qualities. In the resurrection appearances and at Pentecost, the entire community experienced the powerful gift of the continuing presence of the power, the life, the Spirit which had been with Jesus. And this gift began to manifest itself specifically and powerfully through miraculous gifts of speaking, of sharing, and of fellowship.

It was Paul who emphasized in a special way *charismata,* which literally means gifts of *charis,* which in Greek denotes God's unmerited love to us. *Charismata* then are nothing other than God's gifts of love to us. Particular gifts such as speaking in tongues and celibacy may be given to individual believers. Featured even more prominently are the manifestations of grace given for the good of the community of faith. Prophecy was such a gift mentioned frequently by Paul. Paul also regarded apostles, teachers, and prophets as gifts to the church. The greatest gift of all is the gift of love. Whether to the individual or the entire body, the purpose of the gifts is to bring new life. Such power, gifts, and life constitute the presence of the Holy Spirit in the biblical message.

The Early Brethren and the Spirit

Some Brethren who identify closely with the contemporary "Spirit" movement claim that the early Brethren were charismatics. They point to the Danish Brethren, who do identify with European charismatic manifestations, for support of their position. The response to this claim as spelled out in the following pages will be both a yes and a no. Inasmuch as the Brethren imbibed the flavor of German Pietism out of which they came, they were very much part of a movement emphasizing the necessity of Christian experience. Like members of many new movements, the early Brethren were full of life, and vitally interested in the Holy Spirit. Their zeal and enthusiasm were cited by observers.

One such observation was penned by a Radical Pietist immigrant from Germany in 1750.[1] This author leaves us a sharply critical yet informative caricature of four meetinghouses: Quaker, Mennonite, Brethren, and Ephrata, which he literarily places on a main intersection of a certain beautiful city, obviously Philadelphia. In the best constructed building were those who "conducted their meetings in great quiet . . . were modest and kind to each other. . . . did not preach unless led by the Spirit, women as well as men . . . ." Their dress was modest, neat and of the best of material, removing their hats for no one. They placed great emphasis upon the inner substance. The author concludes: "These people are the most powerful and the richest in the city." It is obvious he was describing the Quakers.

The house on another corner had no special appearance. "It seemed to be rather old as it was patched in many places." Above the door was written: "Because we lack the power of the word, we content ourselves with the dead letter." Following this barb, the author continued in the same vein: These "are upright in their conduct. They wear plain clothing. Proud colors may not be worn by them. Most of the men wear beards. When they are grown they are baptized. A little water is poured over their heads. Their meetings are often very sleepy affairs." Though we know of Alexander Mack's respect for the Mennonites, this caricature matches another more negative reference to them as "deteriorated Baptists."

The author describes another house which struck the eye because of its beautifully painted color. "Over the door was a lamp which had been knocked over, with this inscription above it: 'We sing and preach with great outcry, if only the spirit could be thereby.'" In case you have hastily jumped to the conclusion that here the critic is describing the folk at Ephrata, follow carefully his description:

> These people seem rather peaceful and modest in their conduct. Their clothing is middle-class. Most of the men wear beards. They do not tolerate infant baptism. When they become adults and wish to be baptized, they go where water is and have themselves immersed three times. They hold communion or love feasts often. Their meetings are zealous and their preaching and prayer often takes place with great clamor, as if their God could not hear them well. One hymn chases another as if they lack (inner) silence. They teach their cherished truths after the letter.

As a twentieth century writer, I have often assumed that the emotionalism of the Brethren was of a quiet (yet deeply felt) variety, in contrast to the more exuberant outward manifestations of Methodist camp or Pentecostal meetings. Though there is no doubt much validity to this, early Brethren hymns, devotional literature, and obvious Pietist influences suggest that there is some validity to the above references to zeal, clamor, and outcry. Many of us might have been embarrassed, or hopefully thrilled, to have been a part of the early meetings. Perhaps they shared something of the scandal of the first Christians, who are often described by church historians as an enthusiastic sect within first-century Judaism.

Contemporary "Spirit" Movements[2]

Since there are always many who might echo the words of the disciples at Ephesus: "No, we have never even heard that there is a Holy Spirit" (Acts 19:2), we should express our deep gratitude for the fresh blowing of God's gracious Spirit which we have known in contemporary movements. Rooted in the holiness movement of Methodism, Pentecostalism emerged at the beginning of our century to become one of the most dynamic Christian revivals and denominational families of our century. More recently, a new or neo-Pentecostalism has made itself felt within nearly all branches of Christendom. As the older movement adopted its name from the message that Pentecost is repeatable, so present manifestations within the churches have identified often with the label "charismatic," from Paul's focus on *charismata* or gifts of the Spirit. Classical Pentecostals criticize the new charismatics for their feeling that they can have the experience of the baptism of the Holy Spirit without changing basic beliefs and church affiliation and for their tendencies to have their most meaningful experiences outside the circles of their own churches. A lively debate continues in both old and new Pentecostalism concerning the normative nature of speaking in tongues. Many of us who are not as closely identified can join Pentecostals and charismatics in affirming the movement as a genuine manifestation of the Spirit of God renewing the church.

Although most observers of the contemporary scene point to errors and dangers as well as to contributions of the "Spirit" movement, it is well to focus first on the latter. One finds biblical evidences of dynamic spiritual life in many churches related to the movement, churches which once seemed tired or even dead. Here is a belief that with God all things are possible. The promises of God to the early Christians in Acts can be claimed today. Though not universally the case, some congregations have experienced a renewal of life and a deepening of fellowship. The priesthood of all believers becomes a reality, members becoming participants in worship instead of mere onlookers. Christians really do care for one another and are not ashamed to express their love in embraces, their joy in dancing, and their concerns through intercessory prayer. A genuine new manifestation of ecumenism has come into being as Christians from many backgrounds respond to the gift of unity in the Spirit.

In a recent book, Michael Green, who does not identify as a charismatic and critiques the movement biblically, nevertheless offers the following positive evaluation:

> I believe it has done much more good than harm. I believe that it has emphases which the modern churches will neglect at their peril. It has taught us to believe in God's reality and his ability to break into the even tenor of our lives with the invading power of his Spirit. It has taken the doctrine of the Spirit off the dusty shelf and put the person of the Spirit right in the heart of the living room. It has taken the formality, the stuffiness, the professional domination, the dreary predictability out of worship, and made it living, corporate, uplifting, and joyful. It has recognized the variety of gifts God has given to his people, discovered some which had been forgotten for a long time. . . . . It has brought together in intimate fellowship men and women of the most diverse backgrounds. It has driven the silent Christians into bearing joyous and courageous witness to their Lord. . . . It has opened the floodgates to prayer and praise in many a heart that had run dry.[3]

In some places where I myself have encountered the "Spirit" movement, I have discerned from my perspective the powerful presence and activity of God. In other places, I found such bitterness and a spirit of divisiveness that I wanted to shake the dust off my feet as I walked away. It should be remembered that like most movements which attract great numbers, the charismatic movement exhibits a great amount of pluralism. It is impossible to place all charismatics in the same theological basket. When one experiences fractured relationships and disunity in the body as a result of charismatic activity, it must be kept in mind that there are two possible causes. Responsibility can sometimes be laid on the self-righteousness of those who testify to a second experience or who claim that certain gifts are required for all. But responsibility must also be taken by some of us who often react defensively because of our fear of what a powerful awakening of the Spirit might do to our comfortable lukewarm faith.

It is true that not all signs of enthusiasm or outbursts of emotionalism should be attributed to the direct activity of God's Spirit. But contemporary movements of many kinds certainly have contributed to freeing many of us in such a way as to allow the Holy Spirit to come in fresh ways and with new power. My own testimony points to how I was changed through participation in the civil rights and peace movements. Some of what the Blacks identify as "soul" rubbed off on me. This first came to my consciousness in a dramatic way while watching the Southern Christian Leadership Conference film on the life of Martin Luther King, Jr. The film featured the preaching of King and the enthusiastic responses of congregations in the setting of the black church.

As I watched, my memory took me back to my own childhood. It was necessary for us to drive through black neighborhoods on our way to and from church. Since the service in a little Negro church lasted longer, we would stop on a summer evening, rolling our car windows down when the church windows were up. Enjoying what we heard, especially the singing, we nevertheless were filled with a kind of patronizing spirit, one of looking down our noses at the same time we felt a sense of authenticity. We reasoned: "That's the way those black folk are, emotional. If they were more intelligent like we, then they would worship in a more dignified, civilized way like we do."

Many years later, however, in the theater, I realized that my mood had changed from one of superiority to envy. As I watched the scenes from the worship services in which there was such a vital and genuine participation on the part of the worshipers to the powerful message of the preacher, I wished that I belonged to a congregation and a church in which there was more of this kind of spontaneous, warm, genuine, communal manifestation of the Spirit.

The Holy Spirit and
the First Person of the Trinity

Whenever any fundamental doctrine of the· faith is

neglected, a movement will usually emerge to help revive that particular emphasis for the entire church. We have seen that this may be the contribution of many manifestations of the "Spirit" movement in recent decades. There is another side, however, to the story. In most cases, it becomes important to have a corrective to the corrective. In this case any overemphasis on the Third Person of the Trinity needs to be checked by the truths of the First and Second Persons. Our next chapter will focus on the necessity to know the Spirit of Christ in formulating christological tests for certain spirit phenomena. Here we will point to the importance of keeping in our consciousness the God who is beyond our experience, who is transcendent Judge and sovereign over all.

Whenever we know powerful manifestations of the Spirit and the gifts of the Spirit in our midst, we may be tempted to want to capture the Spirit in such a way as to program it for others. Whenever any one of us has a great experience, we are tempted to feel that everyone else has to have the experience. It is so wonderful that it has happened to me, that I want it to happen to each and every person I meet in exactly the same way.

At a large Brethren charismatic gathering at Valparaiso, Indiana, a charismatic minister warned against this tendency by telling a story about a brother who fell in a well. In his frantic desperation, he made many promises to God about how he would change if his life were spared. He was found. A rope was thrown into the pit. The brother was rescued, and he did keep his promises. The event became the basic turning point in his life. He was so thrilled about what had happened to him that he began to go around pushing anyone he could into wells! Charismatics and zealous religion converts are not the only ones to display this tendency. Professors who have had a good experience in their academic pilgrimages sometimes are zealous in their insistence that their students should attend the same graduate schools and do it in exactly the same way. Parents who are satisfied with their own pilgrimage often insist that their children need to have identical experiences.

Though not entirely bad, this type of thinking often overlooks that the God who is beyond our particular experiences can come in other ways to other persons. The gospel of John, in speaking of the work of the Spirit, maintains that "the wind blows where it will, and you hear the sound of it, but you do not know whence it comes or whither it goes." (John 3:8). The basic question which all of us need to ask in reference to our Christian experience is, simply, "Do we fall in love with our experience of God or with the God who gave that experience?"

The focus on Christian experience, in reaction to lifeless religion, often results in what is called anti-intellectualism. An emotional experience seems to eliminate the necessity to dedicate reason. Testimonies often downgrade learning and intellectual leanings. Experience and reason are often polarized in such a way as to refuse to let reason be a valid part of experience. The sense of joy and freedom to express emotions which accompanied the coming of the life-giving Spirit should not lead us to overlook the utterance of wisdom and of knowledge which are also listed by Paul as gifts of the Spirit (1 Cor. 12:8). The first commandment remains that we are to love God with *all* our *minds* as well as with all of our hearts and souls. A Pentecostal scholar, Walter Hollenweger, gives a beautiful analysis of the place of emotions in the Christian faith. He maintains that "emotionalism consists of the seeking and stimulation of emotions as ends in themselves, and not as the byproducts of real experience in truth and in God." Nevertheless, he asserts: "Any genuine experience with the living God will leave an emotional wake in man's psyche. This is not emotionalism but man's being humanized again by the liberating Spirit of God."[4]

When the Spirit brings life in concrete ways, there is yet another temptation, namely, that of wanting to manipulate or control the working of the Spirit. There can be such an enthusiastic desire to participate in the activity of the Spirit as to forget that it is God's work rather than ours. I once heard a story, which is similar to many which circulate in charismatic circles. It was used at the conclusion of a sermon as a way of giving power to everything else that had been said. A brother was critically ill in the hospital. His family called the pastor, requesting that the congregation pray for him. As the congregation gathered the next Sunday morning, they participated fervently in a prayer for their brother. The time was exactly twenty minutes past eleven. Later that same day toward evening, a member of the family contacted the pastor, reporting a sudden turn for the better. Their father dramatically improved from that time and continued in a recovery which was miraculous to the family and remarkable to the doctor. Upon hearing the news, the first immediate response of the pastor was: "What time did the change occur?" The answer came back: "It was twenty minutes past eleven."

The story was one to evoke the spontaneous praise of God. For this reason, the more several of us reflected on the story the more we felt that the pastor had been wrong in his initial response. He should have first joined in praising God for the healing of the brother. His immediate reaction revealed that he was too anxious to relate what God had done with what the congregation had done. The truth is that God could have healed the brother at twenty minutes before eleven had he wished, or at some other time. We are often too eager to set it up in such a way that we might share credit for the work of God. It is true that we are promised by our Lord that we will do his works, even "greater works than these." Jesus adds: "If you ask anything in my name, I will do it" (John 14:12-14). In the Bible, however, the God who so cares and is close remains too big for us ever to get our arms completely around. The foolishness of God's ways ever remain wiser than the wisdom of ours. In the next chapter we will note that to ask in the name of Jesus is to pray in his Spirit, the Spirit of one who prayed, "Nevertheless not my will, but thine, be done" (Luke 22:42).

The Gift of Tongues: A Case Study

No issue gets at the heart of the debate about our tendencies to want to control or domesticate the Spirit as much as the phenomenon of *glossolalia,* speaking in tongues. Traditional Pentecostalism affirms that speaking with tongues as the Spirit gives utterance is the initial physical evidence of the baptism of the Holy Spirit. It thus becomes the sign of whether one truly has received the fullness of the Holy Spirit. This particular gift of the Spirit then becomes normative, which means that it should become part of the experience of every believer who truly wants to be filled with the presence of the Holy Spirit.

This special association of tongues as the evidence of the baptism of the Holy Spirit sets up the possibilities for the kind of divisiveness in the body which we have known. Those who have received the gift of tongues as a result of the baptism of the Spirit and regard it to be the initial physical evidence may genuinely feel that they know a level of Christian life not true of others. Consciously and unconsciously they can give the impression that others who lack this experience simply are not as much in the Spirit or as complete Christians. And those who have not had the experience can either feel they are still second-class Christians or become angry because others may so regard them even if they do not so classify themselves.

It is important to know that the "Spirit" movement is divided on this issue. The mainline Pentecostal movement in the twentieth century has for the most part regarded speaking in other tongues as normative. Many Pentecostals, however, will be quick to point out that this gift is not the summit of Christian experience but rather the beginning of Christian service. It must point beyond itself to Christ and his word and must lead to a life of Christian holiness. Some, not all, neo-Pentecostals or charismatics reject the idea that the gift of tongues should be normative for all Spirit-filled Christians. This is expecially true among European charismatics and among most of the charismatic interpreters within Roman Catholicism.

Because of the many differences of opinion and the complications of biblical interpretation of the primary passages which deal with this issue, it was my plan to shy away from the discussion of tongues as much as possible. However, in reading recent biblical studies which deal with this gift, both by non-charismatics and charismatics, I have been simply amazed at the degree of agreement in terms of biblical interpretation which I have found. So much so that I am about to proclaim such to be the work of the Spirit and to insist that New Testament Brethren should be open to this consensus, regardless of which side we have taken in reference to the charismatic movement.

The Validity of Tongues. Although it may be more difficult to come to any agreement as to what speaking in or with tongues really involves, there is much evidence in the New Testament that early Christians did it. This is the first major point of agreement in the consensus I have mentioned. Strong prejudices which would attempt to rule out tongue-speaking from authentic Christian experience cannot find support from a study of biblical references. Before attempting to substantiate the validity of tongues, it may be helpful to list the main possibilities concerning what speaking in tongues really involves.

(1) Many have felt that what was really involved at Pentecost was a miracle of hearing instead of a miracle of speaking (Acts 2:8). In Christ persons from different ethnic and national backgrounds were nevertheless able to understand one another. In this way Pentecost becomes a wonderful reversal of the confusion of Babel.

(2) Others have insisted that "to speak in other tongues" (Acts 2:4) is to have one's tongue used by God to speak another language not known to the speaker, one which can be understood by others who are acquainted with that language.

(3) In many passages it is most likely that *glossolalia* involves the abandoning of conscious control of speech to give oneself over to an ecstatic speech, a babbling, which can only be understood by God or those having the special gift of interpretation.

(4) Others have maintained that in the Hebrew idiom "to speak with other tongues means nothing other than to speak with excitement, vigorously, and with feeling."[5]

Whether any one of these completely describes the biblical phenomena or whether *glossolalia* in different passages might actually encompass more than one of the above options, the fact of and value of the experience cannot be eliminated from a biblical perspective. Many point to the value of a kind of catharsis which is involved when one lets go so God can take over. Glossolalic speech may become a good medium for the expression of joy or sorrow. In such a case the use of tongues may be similar to what someone else feels in spontaneous dancing. As one who has not experienced or especially sought this particular gift, I have attempted to think of personal experiences which may be the most similar. Often, when filled with joy or experiencing a spirit of thanksgiving for the gift of life, I have run, leaped into the air, and attempted to see how many times I could turn around before coming down, an experience which I used to be more adept at than in these later years!

Richard Baer, a Quaker charismatic, has written an interesting essay in which he notes the similarities between Quaker silence, high church liturgical worship, and speaking in tongues.[6] Because of the sameness and automatic nature of the structure of Catholic and Orthodox liturgy, the worshiper is free as in Quaker silence and glossolalic experience to let go, to "flow" with the leading of the Spirit. His thesis is that we insulate ourselves from divine reality as long as we insist on being fully in control. To experience the presence and power of the Spirit of God necessitates a "letting go," a being open to.

In the very passages in which Paul is the most critical of the appropriation of this gift at Corinth, he nevertheless affirms it: "Now I want you all to speak in tongues, but even more to prophesy" (1 Cor. 14:5). "I thank God that I speak in tongues more than you all; nevertheless, in church I would rather speak five words with my mind, in order to instruct others, than ten thousand words in a tongue" (14:18). He concludes by accenting his preference for prophecy, but adding: "Do not forbid speaking in tongues" (14:39).

Tongues Are Not Normative. The second item concerning which there seems to be strong consensus in biblical scholarship is that tongues should not be regarded as normative. At the same time scholars make a case for the validity of *glossolalia,* they place it in the context of the validity of *many* gifts. It is true that the gift of other tongues comes quickly at Pentecost, but so does the gift of sharing one's possessions with others. Pentecostals can cite many passages in which the gift of tongues is associated intimately with the coming of the Spirit, but there are many other passages, for example, Acts 8:14 ff., in which there is no mention of glossolalia in relation to the receiving the Holy Spirit. Brethren have known the problem of arguing wholly from historical precedent. Are we stuck with always choosing our leaders by lot because of the reporting of this practice in the Book of Acts? Paul's teaching stresses strongly that in reference to the body, any inferiority complex is out of place in the household of God. We are to be open to many gifts which are intended for the service of others.

The fact that there was nothing distinctively Christian about the gift of tongues lessened the tendency of the early Christians to make *glossolalia* THE manifestation of the Spirit. As was true of miracles and visions, ecstatic speech was not peculiar to those moved by the Christian Spirit. Such practices were common in many other religious cults of that day. At Corinth, Paul had to deal with the problem because the Corinthians were influenced by their culture in some of these practices. As has often been the case of such manifestations, they need to be used and appropriated in the Spirit of Christ and for the good of the body in order for them to truly be gifts of the Holy Spirit.

Krister Stendahl refutes the tendency to make normative any one gift, affirming that we need to use our imaginations and our biblical study to expand the lists of possible gifts. Even the lists found in Romans, 1 and 2 Corinthians, and Ephesians are not exhaustive. For example, in the gospels we find mentioned one of the most specific gifts of the Spirit promised in the Bible. Since Christians often will be brought before the courts, we are instructed "not to be anxious how . . . to speak . . . or what to say, for what you are to say will be given to you." And it will not be "you who speak, but the Spirit of your Father speaking through you" (Matt. 10:17-20). See Mark 13:11, Luke 12:11 ff. and Luke 21:12-15 for related sayings on how the Holy Spirit will give us what to say when we appear before the authorities. One translation for *Paraclete,* a word John uses for the Spirit, is *comforter*—but an equally valid translation is *advocate* or *attorney*. In a symposium to which Stendahl was invited, he chided his listeners that had they really wanted to gain insight concerning one of the most frequently mentioned gifts in the New Testament, they would have invited one of the Berrigan brothers, who have often been gifted to speak before the authorities because of their faith.[7]

Stendahl likewise stretches one's imagination in his exegesis of the gift of administration. Since he is a dean, he observes that so many wonderful ideas are always squelched with the warning, "This might set a precedent." In such situations he feels that the Spirit's gift is often to inject a "Why not?"

Is it possible that more will join in affirming both the validity of speaking in tongues—and that this gift is not the only sure sign of the possession of the Spirit? If so, it could mean that both charismatics and non-charismatics can live together in peace in the same church. This might mean that the expression of *glossolalia* may be regulated for the sake of the order of the church; it will not mean that such is forbidden. In the words of Michael Green: "We should neither reject speaking in tongues, nor regard it as the be-all and end-all of spirituality."[8] Charismatics will be asking of others concerning this gift: "Why not?" And non-charismatics will be appealing to charismatics to recognize to a greater degree that the Spirit can really blow where God wills.

It will not be enough to approve of the charismatic movement in a benevolent or academic way without making room for the practice of the gifts of tongues and healing in the mainstream of the life of the community. Clark Pinnock declares that for his part, "the New Pentecostal movement has been raised up not to divide the Body on a spurious doctrine of normativeness, but to open our eyes to the diversity of spiritual manifestations of which we have hitherto been unaware."[8] Charismatics will be admonished that they often seek evidence for the presence of the Spirit too eagerly and too often, for we are basically to walk by faith, not by sight (2 Cor. 5:7). On the other hand more of the rest of us will be sensitized to have a greater sense of expectancy concerning the possibilities of the presence, concretions, and gifts of the Spirit. For the Spirit brings life. And we are admonished to "quench not the Spirit" (1 Thess. 5:19).

Chapter 2

THE LORD IS THE SPIRIT

"Now the Lord is the Spirit, and where the Spirit of the
Lord is, there is freedom" (2 Corinthians 3:17)

Testing the Spirits

When the Spirit comes alive in dynamic and personal ways, there is inevitably the question of discernment. How are we to know whether it is really the Holy Spirit or some other spirit? How can we know the true nature of the Spirit?

Personal experiences and the testimonies of others often raise these kinds of questions in special ways. A sister suddenly came by a large amount of money after being deprived of ready access to cash most of her life. At the same time she became deeply involved in prayer, self-realization, and "Spirit" groups. Depending in increasing ways on direct guidance from God, she began to receive "leadings" instructing her to buy two-hundred dollar dresses. At the time I reasoned that a degree of tolerance should be exercised toward her fulfilling hidden dreams of years. But I did wonder whether she should attribute all of this to God. Both as a check on her "leadings" and my suspicions, there is the need to take seriously the biblical admonitions to "test the spirits" (1 Jn. 4:1 ff.). In this chapter and the next we will attempt to discover proper biblical tests for the spirits in order to discover how we might know whether they are of God.

Jesus and the Spirit

As Christians it is important to keep in mind the christological test and definition of the Spirit. When Paul wrote, "the Lord is the Spirit," he was giving one of the basic biblical definitions of the Spirit, namely, Jesus is the Spirit. Biblical scholars do not attempt to make neat distinctions between the Spirit of God, the Spirit of Christ, Christ in you, the Spirit of Jesus, the Holy Spirit, the power of the risen Christ, or simply the Spirit. The shades of differences should not negate the basically synonymous nature of these expressions. We too need to put the Spirit with Jesus and Christ. Concrete expressions of the charismatic Spirit need to be brought to the test of the Christ event.

It is true that the presence of the Spirit was named and defined before the birth of Jesus. The Old Testament literature abounds with references to the Spirit as life, power, authority, judgment, wisdom, morality, and the promise of the coming kingdom. Disciples and interpreters of Jesus came to believe that Jesus had become the bearer of the same Spirit. The fullness and activity of the Spirit was especially evident in the persons and events surrounding his birth. At his baptism the Spirit descended as a dove, a reference which may allude to the Spirit which hovered over the waters in the priestly creation account in Genesis 1:2.[1]

Accompanying the dove was a voice from heaven proclaiming: "Thou art my beloved Son; with thee I am well pleased (Mark 1:11). Some scholars detect in this heavenly message a fusion of different themes, the servant motif from Isaiah 42:1 with the adoptive motif of Hosea 1:1. Whereas the servant motif points to the nature of his ministry, the adopted Son motif suggests his intimate relationship with God as *Abba* (Father). Jesus' usage of this title in prayer appears to have been distinctive, reflecting a new level of intimacy and trust in addressing God in Jewish circles.

For the gospel writers, Jesus became the focus of the Spirit's activity. He was not just a unique bearer of the Spirit; he was the dispenser of the Spirit. Jesus was a charismatic in that he manifested a power and authority not his own. He became a powerful sign and proclaimer of the dawning reign of God's kingdom. By God's power he cast out demons; his healings were a sign of the beginning of a new age. Jesus apparently had visionary experiences, though there is no evidence that he spoke in tongues. Ever after, Jesus stamps a new character on the Spirit. It is to be called the Spirit of Jesus. In the resurrection appearances, the life-giving Spirit is equated with the risen Christ.

According to the early church, the same God and Spirit of God present in the life of Israel and even more fully in Jesus came again in fullness at Pentecost to Christian believers. The task of the Paraclete, comforter and interpreter, was to universalize the presence of Jesus in the hearts of the disciples. The function of the Spirit was not to bring some new revelation but to bear witness to the living Christ. As with Jesus, when we cry "'Abba, Father,' it is the Spirit himself bearing witness with our spirit that we are children of God" (Rom. 8:15-16). Through this witness of the Spirit we know of our own adoption.

It is the Spirit which gives the gift of repentance leading to life. The true mark of the Spirit occurs when anyone can genuinely make the confession that "Jesus is Lord" (1 Cor.

12:3). It is the Spirit which comes to accompany Christian baptism. The Spirit gives freedom. We receive power to "live in the Spirit, walk in the Spirit" (Gal. 5:24). "If any man does not have the Spirit of Christ, he does not belong to Christ" (Rom. 8:9). A Christian is one who receives the Spirit of Christlikeness, being characterized by the fruit of the Spirit, which is love, joy, peace, patience, kindness, faithfulness, gentleness, self-control" (Gal. 5:22). For Paul the community itself manifests the power of God. The Spirit is recognizable where the community manifests the character of Christ. Johannine thought does not focus on the charismatic community in the same manner as Paul, but there too the Spirit affords direct continuity between Jesus and believers.

The Second and Third Persons
in Christian History

The first large ecumenical council at Nicea in A.D. 325 dealt with the Arian controversy about the nature of Christ. Rejecting the Arian tendency to make Christ distinct and subordinate, the gathering affirmed the equality of the person of Christ in the Godhead. It remained for the Eastern Cappadocian Fathers to lead a crusade in the fourth century which was to result in giving the same status to the Holy Spirit. This was achieved at the second ecumenical council, meeting at Constantinople in 381. When we speak of Christ and the Holy Spirit as persons we should remember that such a translation may be misleading, because the word *person* for us implies much more distinctiveness and individuality than was true of either the Greek or Latin roots.

Though the Council declared the equality of the persons, the differences are important to keep in mind as a corrective whenever we neglect one of the persons of the Trinity. The images of the Spirit as wind and fire point to the free, spontaneous, yet powerful and universal effects of the activity of God. On the other hand the focus on Christ as *Logos,* rational Word, reveals the understanding, clarity, and consistency of God's nature. We shall see that it should be possible to recognize the activity of God in both the inexplicable as well as what can be explained.

In Christian history there has been a long debate concerning the idea of the procession of the Holy Spirit. The basis for this controversy is found in the fifteenth chapter of John, which has Jesus saying: "But when the Counselor comes, whom I shall send to you from the Father, even the Spirit of truth, who proceeds from the Father, he will bear witness to me" (v. 26). In this verse the Spirit is said to proceed from God, at the same time it is promised that Christ will send the Spirit. The churches of Eastern Orthodoxy, following the earliest ecumenical creeds, believe in the procession of the Holy Spirit from the First Person of the Godhead alone. In the Western Church, first in Spain in the sixth century and in Rome in the eleventh century, the *filioque* clause, "and from the Son," was added. The inclusion of this clause in the creed without the presence of the representatives of the entire church was resented by Christians in the East. It became one of the factors, among others, which helped to precipitate the great schism of the church in 1054, a division between Eastern Orthodoxy and Roman Catholicism, which continues to this day.

What difference does it make whether we say that the Spirit comes from the Father alone or from the Father and the Son? Is such a mere quibbling over words? Though the debate has often been at that level, there is something here which, no doubt, has made a difference in Christian life. In refusing to relate the Spirit as intimately to the Son, the Eastern Church has been much more open to mysticism, which usually points to the more direct access of the believer to God. Western piety, while not entirely without mystical streams, has generally been characterized by a greater ordering of the spiritual life by Christ's body, the church. John Macquarrie lists a few arguments in favor of both views. The Eastern emphasis makes it clear that the activity of the Spirit is as wide as creation. As the Spirit was actively present before the coming of Jesus, so we can be open to the freedom of the Spirit to be active outside the specifically Christian community and tradition. Moreover, to argue that the Spirit proceeds from two sources may be to have two gods instead of one. The East has also felt that the West has subordinated the Spirit to the Son, thereby leading to the great neglect of the doctrine of the Holy Spirit.

Macquarrie, in listing the possible advantages of refusing to think of the Spirit apart from the Son, feels that the West has a slightly stronger case. It is by stressing this relationship between the Spirit and the Son that definite content is added to our understanding of the Spirit. The Spirit thereby is understood primarily in a personal way. When the Spirit is symbolized only as wind or fire, he or she can be translated as an "it," an impersonal force invading human lives. As already noted, the Western view guards against separating Logos and Spirit. This preserves the need for both inspired understanding and guided emotionalism. The western view, according to Macquarrie, provides a criterion for discerning or testing the spirits, something which remains as necessary for us as it was for the New Testament church.

The above analysis does not mean that there have not been many Spirit-filled movements in the West. Medieval reform and mystical groups, much of the Radical Reformation, German Pietism, English Quakerism, and Methodist and Evangelical Revivals all represented a strong accent on the presence and power of the Holy Spirit. The same trinitarian tension which was a part of the great schism has also appeared in Western Christendom. In his Table-Talk, Martin Luther related an interesting personal experience in order to stress his bias for depending on the Word, namely, Christ, over any special visions or revelations:

> On Good Friday last, I being in my chamber in fervent prayer, contemplating with myself, how Christ my Savior on the cross suffered and died for our sins, there suddenly appeared upon the wall a bright vision of our Saviour Christ with the five wounds, steadfastly looking upon me. as if it had been Christ himself corporally. At first sight, I thought it had been some celestial revelation, but I reflect that it must needs be an illusion and juggling of the devil, for Christ appeared to us in his Word, and in a meaner and more humble form; therefore I spake to the vision thus: Avoid thee, confounded devil: I know no other Christ than he who was crucified, and who in his Word is pictured and presented unto me. Whereupon the image vanished, clearly showing of whom it came.[3]

Inasmuch as the early Brethren were influenced by earlier sixteenth century Anabaptism and late seventh century Pietism, they were a part of a milieu with a greater theology of experience. These movements were more inclined to special emphases on the Holy Spirit than to the strict connection of the

Spirit to the Word or to the Scriptures characteristic of Martin Luther and John Calvin respectively. Evangelical Anabaptists and the later Mennonites did check any charismatic excesses by adherence to the life and teachings of Jesus. Philipp Spener however, the father of German Pietism, was more open to mystical influences, special revelations, and many other types of charismatic manifestations, though he emphasized that all such experience needs to be tested by Christ, the Scriptures, and the Church. It was in Radical Pietist circles that the Spirit often became separated, so that it was felt that the entire Bible could be found within one's soul. This stress on the inner word, sometimes to the exclusion of outward forms and scripture, may have dominated some of the circles which the Brethren left in order to form a more visible church.

Surrounded by Radical Pietists at Schwarzenau, including the Community of True Inspiration (the later Amana colonies), Alexander Mack was forced to deal with this issue. In the early Brethren leader's conversational writing with his son, the son asks about the many Christians who claim that in the new covenant all of the law of God is written in their hearts. In his answer Mack reveals a belief that such talk contains some truth but is also intermingled with lies. Supporting both the work of the Holy Spirit in the writing of the canon as well as in the hearts of believers, Mack concludes: "This law which is inwardly written by the Spirit of God is completely identical with that which is outwardly written in the New Testament."[4] On the one hand he seemed to be more open to extra-biblical activities of the Spirit than someone like John Calvin, who identified closely the inner testimony of the Holy Spirit with rightly interpreting the Bible. On the other hand, Mack was affirming that all inner revelations must be tested by the New Testament. If this test is combined with the strong *imitatio Christi* (imitation of Christ) theme which was present in Mack and the early Brethren, there is real support for formulating the Brethren view of authority in this way: *All charismatic knowledge and experiences need to be tested by the community as it gathers around the scriptures to discern the mind of Christ.*

Testing the Spirits

But do not trust any and every spirit, my friends; test the spirits, to see whether they are from God, for among those who have gone out into the world there are many prophets falsely inspired. This is how we may recognize the Spirit of God: Every spirit which acknowledges that Jesus Christ has come in the flesh is from God, and every spirit which does not thus acknowledge Jesus is not from God (1 Jn. 4:1-3, NEB).

Now concerning spiritual gifts, brethren, I do not want you to be uninformed. You know that when you were heathen, you were led astray to dumb idols, however you may have been moved. Therefore I want you to understand that no one speaking by the Spirit of God ever says "Jesus be cursed!" and no one can say "Jesus is Lord" except by the Holy Spirit (1 Cor. 12:1-3).

From these passages it is clear that one of the primary tests of the Spirit is simply: "Does it point to Jesus as Lord?" In the church at Corinth there were members who in their spiritual frenzy shouted, "Jesus be cursed!" In that church generally there seemed to be many with a preference for the lower spiritual gifts over the higher ones, or at least for those somewhat associated with the idolatry of the pagan world. Paul wanted to say strongly that the test must be whether spiritual gifts truly build up the kind of life manifested in Jesus Christ. Then as today there were many who tended to glorify their experience and call attention to phenomena or signs and not to Christ. The really crucial mark of the Spirit's presence is not just any kind of new power and life, but life and power which reflects the Spirit of our Lord, which thereby confesses that Jesus is Lord.

We live in a day when we can be blown about by many winds of doctrine. In recent years we have experienced a great proliferation of fortunetellers, astrologers, exorcists, witches, gurus, all more available than ever through the media and contemporary mobility. We have seen the great success of Transcendental Meditation, Neo-Hindu cults, Scientology, new mystery cults, and many others. Even in the Christian world there is such a variety of celebrities in popular religion that it is easy to become a faddist or just plain confused. I have encountered brothers and sisters whose trust level is higher with a popular religious person because of frequent relationship through the tube than with me, one who shares a common ethnic Christian heritage. I confess that such is painful. In our pluralistic society, how are we to keep from being tossed to and fro by the many winds of doctrine?

Though it is impossible to give an easy and pat answer to this concern, it is worth looking at. The christological test is essential. Though I do not as automatically name as demonic the current interest in psychic powers as do some of my charismatic friends, I do believe that such phenomena need to be tested. For example, if someone has been gifted with E.S.P. (extra sensory perception) or seems to intuitively know when fortune or danger is imminent, the appropriate response remains "so what?" Not that one is laughing at authentic psychic abilities or at phenomena which scientists may indeed know much more about in the future. Rather, it is to ask the question: "To what is this dedicated?" Is it to be utilized in the Spirit of Jesus? If one can communicate without benefit of telephone, telegraph or satellites, it is still important to examine what one says and the spirit in which it is said. The same is true of other abilities. We can rejoice if someone is gifted with a high I.Q. But high intelligence can be dedicated to the devil, to the worst kind of manipulation of other persons. Or, a keen mind can be dedicated to the Lord. Paul suggests to the Corinthians that the Spirit is involved as much in how a talent is used as in bestowing the talent. This defines the nature of Christian egalitarianism. We are not all equally gifted. But we can all be open to the use of the gifts we have by the Spirit, the Spirit of Jesus, the Way of love.

Some may feel that in dealing with the right dedication of our abilities, we may be missing the essential teaching of being open to the coming of God's power and Spirit to work in and through us. Even here, however, such signs and wonders need to be tested to discern whether they point to themselves or to God. Like Luther in the above illustration, we need to test whether our desire for celestial revelation may or may not be a rejection of the Way God has come through the Word and the community of faith. In delving into phenomena which attempt to demonstrate the immortality of the soul, we need to examine whether our curiosity may be overriding the promises of God. The biblical prejudice against soothsayers and astrology suggests that the promises of God are meant to eliminate preoccupation with all of the details of the future and to allow God's future to be lived as a powerful force in the present. We may receive personal "leadings" and guidance from God. But these need to be tested as to whether they are authentically from God or represent rationalizations of our own wishes. Are powerful happenings the manifestation of the human spirit or the Holy Spirit? Such need to be tested by the Spirit of Christ.

Now, the question becomes, how are we to know the Spirit of Christ? Since we are dealing with God's Spirit and not ours, since we are attempting to discern the nature of a person rather than an object which can be examined, we are destined as Paul points out to "know in part" and "to see in a mirror dimly" (1 Cor. 13:12). Though we read the same Gospels, Christians continue to discern differing pictures of Jesus and the nature of His Spirit and Way. But we can know in part, if not completely. Paul in the same chapter suggests another way to give content to the testing of the spirits. In between chapters discussing the gifts of the Spirit, Paul speaks of a more excellent way, the way of love. In the love chapter of 1 Corinthians 13 as well as in Romans 12, love for Paul is *charisma,* a gift. All of the other gifts are nothing other than God's gifts of love. We have made the case that no one of the usual gifts of the Spirit should be made normative or required of every Christian. Here, we take that back. There is one which should be received by all, namely, the gift of love. Since Jesus in his crucifixion remains the supreme example of one who lived and died for others, this kind of self-giving love remains the supreme test of all other gifts. Paul applies this test to some of the most popular gifts at Corinth. If one has the gift of prophecy, the gift of powerful faith so as to be able to work miracles, or the gift of sharing, and does not use such a gift in the Spirit of Jesus, of love, it is nothing (1 Cor. 13:1-2).

Paul's focus on love does not make possible any scientific test. It should, however, help simplify what for some has become too complicated. If you, like the author, benefited early from the love of a mother who imbibed from the stream of love of the community going back to Jesus, you were receiving the Spirit of Jesus, the Holy Spirit. If you have experienced the special love and care of brothers and sisters in the body of Christ, you have received the Holy Spirit. If you have known an acceptance beyond what you feel you deserve, you have known the grace or gift of the Holy Spirit.

Theology of Glory and Theology of the Cross

In Christendom theologies of glory have often been contrasted with theologies of the cross. *Theologia gloriae* focuses on the glory, majesty, power, miracles, and victory of God. *Theologia crucis* focuses on the knowledge of God which comes through the lowly birth of Jesus, his suffering, and death. Luther, who preached the latter, contrasted the way we would have done it, having Jesus come in the splendor of an earthly king, with the way God did it, having Jesus born as a baby in a barn smelling with manure. He criticized our desire to know God through the miraculous rather than through his lowliness and suffering. Others say that the theology of glory caters to our selfish needs to receive help from God; whereas the theology of the cross calls us to participate in the suffering of God for the sins of the world.

As with many theological debates, theologians end up saying that we need elements of both. As some of us may not be open enough to what God can powerfully do through us for the coming kingdom, others have forgotten that true power comes from patient endurance in suffering. One of the faults of the charismatics at Corinth was that they were so infatuated with the idea of the fullness of the Spirit as to be somewhat allergic to the theology of the cross. Paul needed, therefore, to write strongly against their boasting. He felt the need to preach Christ crucified as a corrective to their kind of emphasis on the Spirit. He contrasted their being puffed up in their claim to be full of the Spirit with the condition of others, including himself.

> We are fools for Christ's sake, but you are wise in Christ. We are weak, but you are strong. You are held in honor, but we in disrepute. To the present hour we hunger and thirst, we are ill-clad and buffeted and homeless, and we labor, working with our own hands. When reviled, we bless; when persecuted, we endure; when slandered, we try to conciliate; we have become, and are now, as the refuse of the world, the offscouring of all things (1 Cor. 4:10-13).

Spirit christology is only realistic when seen in the light of the trinitarian theology of the cross. Some charismatics today claim that since God always desires health, such will be granted if we have enough faith. A young brother revealed his one-sided focus on the theology of glory or success in his rejection of the

Brethren emphasis on simplicity. He explained that if he lived simply he would refuse to give evidence of God's blessings and thereby fail to testify to the gifts of God. These claims are contrary to many biblical accounts. For example, the Spirit not only convinces Paul that imprisonment and afflictions awaited him if he journeyed to Jerusalem, but bound him to carry through in the decision (Acts 20:22, 23). Christian life and discipleship may involve suffering. Though the theology of glory or resurrection is one which promises ultimate victory, the assurance of the presence of the Spirit does not lead to an escape into dream worlds beyond the realities of this one. Rather, the Spirit often sends us more deeply into Christ's sufferings.

The desire to focus exclusively on the victorious power of the Spirit is seen sorrowfully in the following story. A brother accompanied by his charismatic group attended a Kathryn Kuhlman meeting. Before her death the well-known faith healer claimed to have the gift of discerning God's healings, more than the gift of healing itself. She did discern at this meeting that the brother had been healed. He and the prayer group came home rejoicing. They joyfully shared their testimony with the church family and with many others. Because they all had told the story so many times, they failed to acknowledge there was anything happening when the illness returned and their loved one began to get worse. Even those in the family and other friends who sensed what was happening would say nothing about it, for fear of contradicting the strong expressions of faith which had accompanied the many testimonies. Everybody had to pretend their brother remained well even while he was dying. His death was a shattering experience for the charismatic group and his family. This kind of theology of resurrection, which attempted to deny the reality of suffering instead of recognizing that victory can come through suffering, led to a kind of situation where it was not possible for a brother to face realistically his own death. He and his loved ones were denied the privilege of discussing death and their plans and hopes for the future in the light of the Christian faith.

Such a refusal to recognize the possibility of suffering and death, even for the most devout Christian, often goes along with a tendency to manipulate God's Spirit in terms of what we might call a one-to-one theology. Such a view maintains a one-to-one relationship between our faith and what God will do for us. I was privileged to live near Brother William Beahm, long-time dean of Bethany Seminary, during some of the last months he suffered so intensely from a terminal cancer. He not only had to endure much pain, but also the good intentions of many brothers and sisters. Many letters came with the advice: "If you have faith, William, you will be healed." Perhaps the writers were not thinking of the full implications of what they wrote. For the other side of what they shared turned out to be: "If you do not get better, it will be because you do not have enough faith."

Can we really bind God in this way, however? Concerning sin, grace is the reality that God often forgives us beyond what we deserve. Concerning suffering, there is certainly no one-to-one relationship between what Jesus suffered on the cross and what he deserved. Any theology of glory which promises "Whatever you ask in my name, I will do it" (John 14:3) needs to remember that the christological test is built into those very words. It should be kept in mind in interpreting other verses, even those like John 15:7, where it is not explicit. To ask in the name of Jesus is to ask in the Spirit of one who prayed, "Nevertheless not my will, but thine, be done" (Luke 22:42).

Chapter 3

THE FELLOWSHIP OF THE HOLY SPIRIT

"The grace of the Lord Jesus Christ and the love of God
and the fellowship of the Holy Spirit
be with you all" (2 Corinthians 13:14).

Spirit and Community

In the Bible there is a close relationship between the Spirit of God and the community of faith. Ezekiel indicates the gift of the Spirit to the people in one of his "Thus saith the Lord" passages: "A new heart I will give you (Israel), and a new spirit I will put within you . . . and cause you to walk in my statutes and be careful to observe my ordinances" (Ez. 36:26, 27). The special outpouring of the Spirit at Pentecost is a vital part of the story of the birth of the Christian Church. Ever since, the doctrines of the church and the Spirit have been intimately related in Christian statements of faith and books of dogma. God's creation utterance: "Let *us* make man in *our* image; after *our* likeness" (Gen. 1:26) indicates that sociality is rooted in the very heart of God. In the Pauline benediction in 2 Corinthians 13:14 the Greek word for "fellowship" may also be translated "participation in" the Holy Spirit. The corporate dimension of religious experience is basic to Paul's understanding of divine-human relationships. For him it was evident that the gifts of the Spirit and community belong together.

If the Church of the Brethren has any special contribution to make to the "Spirit" movement, it may be to share from its tradition that which highlights the communal definition of the Spirit. We have been influenced by an Anabaptist heritage which has felt that no one can come to God except together with the sister and the brother. The neighbor constitutes an essential element in one's personal redemption. How can any one love God whom we cannot see apart from the love of a brother or a sister who can be seen (1 Jn. 4:20)?

For this reason a few passages may come easier for Brethren than for others. Many have puzzled over the story in Acts 8 of the Samaritans, who "had only been baptized in the name of the Lord Jesus" (v. 16) until Peter and John were sent from the church at Jerusalem. "Then they laid hands on them and they received the Holy Spirit" (v. 17). Some have interpreted this as a proof of a two-step approach to salvation: First we are baptized by water; later we need to be baptized by the Holy Spirit. Others have felt this story to be somewhat strange, one which really does not fit the entire message of the New Testament church. For Brethren, however, the story simply illustrates the truth that we do not have the Spirit apart from relationship with the community of faith.

The Apostle Paul knew one of the most dramatic conversions recorded in biblical narrative in his personal encounter with the living Christ. But it was in connection with his arrival in Damascus and his relationship to the community of faith there that he was filled with the Holy Spirit (Acts 9:1-19). For the Brethren the laying on of hands is a beautiful New Testament symbol to point to the fact that God's Spirit comes to us through the lives of brothers and sisters. This chapter does not need a special Brethren section; rather, each of the chapter topics intersects our heritage at some point.

Baptism and Baptism of the Holy Spirit

We live in a time when many testify to receiving the baptism of the Holy Spirit. Most who so testify were previously baptized by water, either as infants, children, or adults. Many have been active in churches for years. The Spirit-baptism represents a new or second experience. I write this book while living temporarily in Kentucky. The tradition of large numbers here has been to identify themselves as "born again" Christians. Their experience is compared with their first birth from the womb, which is the metaphor of the third chapter of John. But folk are confused now because the current "born again" testimonies so popular in American life point to something else. Whereas previously the new life was contrasted with a life of sin before their first baptism, the new life which comes through the second baptism and the gifts of the Spirit is often set over against that of a lifeless church member. The growing occurrence of the need for a second baptism may be a judgment on the church for a long-time trend to minimize the first experience.

Personally, I have listened to beautiful and genuine testimonies of the baptism of the Holy Spirit. A couple testified that before the baptism they felt it was up to them to save the church and the world. Their baptism meant a "letting go" of their desire to manipulate, so as to trust God to work through all. On the other hand, I have listened to testimonies which worked at contrasting the previous life with the present in such a way as to almost completely negate the wonderful work of the Spirit which I believed I had discerned in their lives before the

Spirit-baptism. I know that I have sometimes displayed a spirit of defensiveness when it has been suggested that I have not received the Holy Spirit, at least in fullness. This defensiveness results from my failure to be open to a need for a greater presence of the Spirit, as well as a distrust of the good intentions of charismatic friends. In some of their testimonies, however, I have sensed unlovely and self-righteous attitudes toward those who do not testify to the same experience. The present situation is one which is fraught by much confusion, misunderstanding, and alienation.

Because of the confusion, it may be important to look at the rootage of the present phenomena in the history of the church. Early eighteenth century Methodism, like German Pietism, placed a great emphasis on the conversion experience even though infant baptism was not repudiated. Both movements also stressed the need for sanctification or continual growth in grace. Unlike the Pietists, however, the Methodists began to allow the possibility of a second special work of grace to actualize this growth. John Wesley in his doctrine of perfection allowed that he knew several who had known such a second experience. his analysis of such an experience, however, remained within the context of his dynamic view of salvation. Entire sanctification was something that you grew into, could lose easily, and which needed to be followed by growth in the Christian life. Though Wesley never claimed the experience for himself and later began to question its efficacy in the lives of some who claimed it, he did open the door to a scheme of salvation which was to mushroom in succeeding generations. It was this doctrine which was revived by the Holiness movement in the nineteenth century, the second work of grace being called entire sanctification, perfection, the second blessing, or a state achieved by "praying through."

Around the turn of the century, the first Pentecostals emerged within the Holiness movement. In fact, in early Pentecostalism the baptism of the Holy Spirit was regarded as the third work of grace, following conversion and entire sanctification. This relationship of Pentecostals to the Holiness movement can be documented by the name of a large denomination which began in the early part of the twentieth century, the Pentecostal Church of the Nazarene. The church soon dropped the first word of its name, when it identified more specifically with the Holiness movement. As it identified with the Holiness emphasis, which featured the second work of sanctification, the Pentecostal movement, reducing the number from three to two, focused on the second work of grace as the baptism of the Holy Spirit.

Many Christians have difficulties with the two-plateau approach to the Christian life. Some from revivalistic and evangelical traditions feel that to focus on a need for a second experience detracts from the initial saving encounter. They believe that those truly converted are already filled with the Holy Spirit. To be a Christian at all is to be baptized by one Spirit. Like others, they feel that it becomes easy to move to a two-level Christianity, in which you have a class of superior Christians. Some do not object to using the word *baptism* to refer to subsequent fillings of the Spirit, but reason that it should not be tied to a tight "second work" scheme.

Roman Catholics deal with the Pentecostal view in a different way by fitting it into their tradition. Charismatic prayer groups within Catholicism present Spirit-baptism as a renewal of one's confirmation. Instead of the new baptism negating previous experiences as so often occurs among Protestants, charismatic experience is a fulfillment and realization of the Spirit which has already been given through the sacramental life of the church. Catholic charismatics, for the most part, are more closely related to the church. Many testify that their experience has renewed their loyalty to the church, deepened their understanding of its basic doctrines, and led to a greater sense of service and mission to the world. Baptism in the Spirit is spoken of as a release of the Spirit which has already been present, rather than as being a new filling. A Roman Catholic nun testifies, for example, that one of the greater gifts she has received has been the gift of a genuine friendship with Mary.[1]

Before struggling with a possible Brethren interpretation, it is appropriate to look at some biblical evidence. One of the passages giving the strongest support to the Pentecostal two-stage baptism is the story concerning the disciples at Ephesus which is found in the first verses of Acts 19. When asked if they had received the Holy Spirit when they believed, the disciples responded that they had never heard that there is a Holy Spirit.

When it was discovered that they had only been baptized into John's baptism, they were baptized again in the name of the Lord Jesus. "And when Paul had laid his hands upon them, the Holy Spirit came on them; and they spoke with tongues and prophesied" (v. 6).

To understand this story, it is important to appreciate its historical setting. Many had received the baptism of John, which was associated with repentance, forgiveness, and participation in a community of expectancy concerning the coming of the kingdom. This movement provided many who became converts to Christianity. Baptism or immersion *by the Spirit* is a phrase used by John and others to point to the difference between his baptism and the coming baptism by Jesus. At Pentecost those who had already received the baptism of John were baptized with the Spirit. After Pentecost only the disciples of John were advised to pray for the baptism of the Holy Spirit. Historically, then, the two experiences refer to a special situation in Jewish circles, where those who had first received the baptism of John later became Christians. The receiving of the Holy Spirit was connected to becoming a part of the Christian fellowship. Such a twofold scheme disappeared as the coming of the Holy Spirit continued to be associated with the initiatory experience of becoming a Christian.[2]

There is hardly any evidence that the Brethren considered a two-stage scheme before encountering the Holiness movement in the nineteenth century. It is important to keep in mind, however, that from the beginning Brethren baptismal practice has included a powerful symbolic act pointing to the presence of the Holy Spirit. Following the threefold immersion in the name of the persons of the Trinity, there is a laying on of hands to symbolize the baptism of the Spirit. Whereas other churches, especially those who baptize infants, separate baptism from confirmation (which comes later), the Brethren join baptism and confirmation in one service. The laying on of hands also means that the Brethren join baptism in water with baptism in the Spirit. In Titus 3:5 we have reference to baptism as both the bath of rebirth and renewal by the Spirit.

In 1747 the Society of Friends circulated a German translation of one of their tracts which criticized those who emphasized outward water baptism. In the same year a Brethren answer appeared which defended baptism, at the same time stressing the importance of the operation of the Holy Spirit:

> . . . even though we indeed firmly maintain out of love to Christ and His true words that no professor of Christ has a right to omit water baptism and to separate it from the work of conversion, still we do not consider water baptism alone the seal of true conversion, rather the gift of the Holy Spirit (Acts 2:36) which is the guarantee and seal of our inheritance (Eph. 1:13-14, 2 Cor. 1:21-22). And if God had separated the baptism of water and spirit from each other, and had given us the choice of the one we wished, then we would not act wisely if we stretched out both our arms for the baptism of the Holy Spirit, neglecting the other. Especially even now when we realize with open eyes that the baptism of Christ was arranged by God himself, yet we are not baptized in water for the sake of the water but rather for the sake of the Holy Spirit, because we know that the Spirit of God, through which we seek to be baptized, has commanded the water baptism, and therefore does not disdain water. . . .
>
> If, however, someone received the water baptism and does not also receive a gift of the Holy Spirit, and is in addition very content with his unblessed water baptism such a one is in a bad condition. Even where Spirit and water are together the water cannot bless the Spirit but the Spirit must bless the water.[3]

Here we can see the Brethren desire to hold water and Spirit baptism together without imbibing any automatic view that water baptism guarantees the baptism of the Holy Spirit.

As suggested by our comments above, the laying on of hands points to and is an act of participating in a relationship with the community of faith. The action embodies the reality of the gift of the Spirit coming to the person through the church. As this relationship becomes real with God and others, it can be claimed that the Holy Spirit has been received. And to so receive the Holy Spirit is an assurance to Brethren that in their baptism they also have been baptized by the Holy Spirit. In the baptismal experience, the believer brings repentance and faith; water baptism is provided by the church; and the Holy Spirit is given by God through both.

But this does not mean that our practice of baptism guarantees the presence of the Holy Spirit. Alexander Mack, Jr. wrote against baptismal regeneration, a belief that baptism in itself saves:

> To say and to pretend that baptism is the means and under this
> pretense to practice baptism and recommend it as the only means
> whereby forgiveness of sins and the Holy Spirit may be given,
> sound exceedingly superstitious and idolatrous beyond measure.[4]

Because of the possibility of a lack of faith, or a later falling from faith, the Brethren did feel that there should be opportunities for renewal type experiences. Because they did not wish to negate the initial relationship, however, they opposed another baptism for those who had been received as adults. For such second or third or additional experiences they thought of occasions like love feasts or anointings. This does not mean that we should not be open to subsequent baptisms with fire (meaning judgment, persecution, or cleansing) and with the Holy Spirit through new laying on of hands. It does mean, however, that we should rejoice in what assurance we have of the gift of the Spirit received earlier—and respond to the call to continue to realize the charismatic fullness of this reality. Such a view is documented by a story which has circulated in several Pennsylvania congregations. A brother, caught up in the fervor of a revival which swept through the churches, asked for baptism. Rising out of the water with an enthusiastic leap, hands high in the air, he shouted, "It is finished!" The elder firmly clamped his hand on the brother's shoulder, admonishing, "No, brother, it's just beginning."

The Spirit Gives Unity

The communal focus of the Spirit is not only seen in relation to *baptism,* but likewise in the frequent New Testament references to *unity.* As Christians we are to be "eager to maintain the unity of the Spirit in the bond of peace" (Eph. 4:3). However the nature of tongues is interpreted, we can agree that at Pentecost there occurred a reversal of the curse of Babel. The Old Testament curse recorded in Genesis resulted in a confusion of tongues; at Jerusalem on the day of Pentecost there occurred an experience of great unity and understanding.

For the rabbis, Pentecost had become the greatest feast of the year. Originally a harvest festival, it later came to be connected with the gift of the law at Sinai. The gift of the law came with a vision of the appearance of God. Such theophanies in the Old Testament were frequently accompanied by wind and fire.

According to a later Jewish tradition, God first offered his law to the nations, and only when they refused did he offer it to Israel. Rabbi Johanan dealt with the problem of language here by saying that God's voice divided into seventy tongues so that all the nations could understand.[5] Inasmuch as the story in Acts points back to Sinai as well as Babel, we have another reversal, this time the universalizing of the gospel for all nations. This became one of the central themes of the Book of Acts. The events at Pentecost became the fulfillment of God's original intention.

In researching the development of the thought of the Brethren between the Revolutionary and Civil Wars, I was struck by their preoccupation with the theme of unity. As new communities became isolated through western migration, the Annual Meeting dealt with divisive issues year after year in an effort to maintain the unity of the Spirit. Because of the teaching that each and every day is sacred, the Brethren had originally rejected many of the traditional holy days of the church year. They ardently met at Pentecost, however, for their biggest love feast and meeting of the year. Though only the Old Orders retain the Pentecost time, the "big" meeting remains as a powerful unifying force in all Brethren groups.

One of the most used and abused unitive texts concerning the Spirit has been that of Paul:

> Now there are varieties of gifts, but the same Spirit; and there are varieties of service, but the same Lord; and there are varieties of working, but it is the same God who inspires them all in every one. To each is given the manifestation of the Spirit for the common good (1 Cor. 12:4-7).

The wonderful unity-in-diversity theme Paul develops has often been violated in ecumenical circles and especially in local congregations. We have been so anxious to keep our institution alive and not lose members, to attempt to affirm everybody by affirming a variety of beliefs and practices, as to misconstrue Paul's intent. Instead of a variety of gifts, service, and working, too often it has been a variety of beliefs, spirits, lords, and gods. There are simply too many passages in the New Testament which appeal to us to be of the same mind and the same Spirit, and which point to one Lord, one baptism, one faith, to be satisfied with a glorification of differences. I do not believe that you find in the Bible a "everybody believe your own thing or do your own thing" method of keeping the unity of the church. A common variation of this in contemporary church life has been the attempt to keep the unity by a "keep your beliefs to yourself" approach. We deal with our differences by refusing to deal with them, for fear of upsetting the "alleged" unity of the church.

Neither, however, does the unitive activity of the Spirit imply an enforced uniformity. The Holy Spirit, the Spirit of our Lord, is not to be found in an approach which is characterized by "everybody believe or do my thing or else." Whereas some err by attempting to maintain institutional unity through doctrinal indifference and individualistic freedom, the opposite temptation is an attempt to preserve it through a rigid and legalistic style. Such often leads to clarity without charity, to laws divorced from the law of love. We are called to be of one heart, mind, and Spirit. But to be of the Spirit is to be together because of love and in love. Nearly every passage which calls for one mind follows with admonitions to love one another, to have compassion for one another, and to keep the bond of peace. Unity remains a gift, in which we can participate but which can never be rigidly enforced. Even Matthew 18:15-20, which allows as a third step that of regarding a brother as a heathen after all else has been tried, is placed in a context in which the preceding verses express God's desire that not one weak member should perish, and the verses which follow command us to forgive seventy times seven.

How might these very principles be applied to the dissensions which surround the presence of the charismatic movement in the life of the church? We need to move beyond a "live and let live" posture. We need to listen to testimonies of charismatics in order to learn why many of our brothers and sisters need new baptisms of the Spirit and in order to be open to new gifts of God's power today. Charismatics need to hear those who testify to the reality of the presence of the Spirit in ways which are different than their style. Together we must be willing to strive together to test the spirits. Rejecting either liberal glorification of differences or conservative legalism, we should rejoice in the varieties of gifts, service, and working which can be dedicated to the same Spirit, Lord, and God. In love, we need to strive for greater unity in the Spirit.

The Communal Test

"One Spirit, one body" implies that if something is truly of the Spirit it will be for the good of the body. In the last chapter we looked at the christological test of the spirits, focusing finally on the gift of love. The test of love meshes readily with the communal test. For we are not graced with spiritual gifts for purposes of personal pride or gratification, for comparing ourselves with others who have less or different gifts. Spiritual gifts are intended for the service of others. They are not given to enhance our good feelings as much as for the edification of our brothers and sisters. Paul's simple test became: "Whatever builds up the body, is of the Spirit." The Spirit makes fellowship. The Spirit enables worship. The Spirit speaks through preaching. The Spirit inspires scripture so that it becomes a living Word. The Spirit leads the congregation to utter the Amen in expressing unity with what has been said in worship.

In writing to the Corinthians Paul had to deal with those who had taken their freedom in Christ to mean that they were free from eating meat offered to idols or free to take off their veils in worship. It was in this context that he said: "All things are lawful, but not all things are helpful. All things are lawful (permissible), but not all things build up. Let no one seek his own good, but the good of the neighbor" (1 Cor. 10:23-24). It was this same principle that Paul applied to an even more basic matter, the way charismata (gifts of the Spirit) were being manifested in the church. Only when such gifts are manifested as expressions of grace, humble selfless love, will the community be benefited. In the lengthy passages which treat this issue (1 Cor. 12—14), the test involving the edification of the community appears again and again. He writes that "to each is given the manifestation of the Spirit for the common good."

Appropriating the analogy of the body, Paul emphasizes the care the members should have for one another. Paul seems to favor prophecy because it can work for "upbuilding, encouragement, and consolation." If someone speaks in tongues, he hopes that another will interpret "so that the church may be edified." He admonishes that if we are really eager for manifestations of the Spirit, we will "strive to excel in building up the church." Generally, at Corinth, he wants all things to be done decently and in order. "For God is not a God of confusion but of peace." For Paul the miraculous is not to be carried away into a disorderly frenzy. The miraculous presence of the Spirit brings order rather than disorder. It is obvious that the test of love in the sense of building up the body is one of the important themes in Pauline thought.

Some studies of the charismatic experience have suggested that it accentuates characteristics which are already present.[6] If a person is loving by nature, becoming a charismatic may mean being graced even more with a loving disposition. But if a person has a history of divisiveness, this may be accentuated. Though containing insights which certain observations seem to verify, such psychological analyses should not be used to negate the charismatic message that God can turn around our lives. The causes of dissension are often difficult to determine. Jesus brought a sword, or division, not because of his divisive nature but because of the reactions of those who felt judged by a loving person. There is often a fine line between whether we are divided because of responses to someone who speaks the truth with love or because someone speaks the truth without love. The gift of discernment may often be the one we need the most. When the Spirit brings power and new life, such power must ultimately effect better understanding and relationships in the body if it is to be truly a manifestation of the Holy Spirit. Charismatic activity *and* responses to such manifestations need to be tested as to whether there is given greater love, clarity, and unity for our lives together.

Special Gifts

A typical Brethren reaction to any list of special gifts is to affirm that all of life is to be lived in conscious dependence upon God's gift of grace, which at any time may permeate attitudes, situations, and relationships. Though this represents the essence of Brethren theology, Brethren should be admonished to remain open to naming special gifts. Brethren tend likewise to be suspicious of the conferring of super-gifts. We prefer the testimony of Paul that "the Spirit helps us in our weakness, interceding for us when we "do not know how to pray as we ought" (Rom. 8:26). Nevertheless, our "humility" should not make us afraid of becoming more alive in the Lord. Though we can prooftext our previous claim that love is to be regarded as a gift of the Spirit (Rom. 4:5), charismatics are right in insisting that this more general and basic gift is different than the more specific gifts listed so frequently in the New Testament.

The purpose of a variety of gifts is that grace may manifest itself in many different ways and in all sorts of circumstances. All of the gifts are to be viewed as gifts for the common good of the body. This, we have seen, provides an important test of the spirits, of the gifts, and of the spirit in which a gift is used. Although Paul prefers some manifestations over others in the community, he basically wants to emphasize that there are many gifts of the Spirit. There is basic equality between the more spectacular and non-spectacular. It is wrong for those who have them to look down their noses on those who do not. On the other hand those who do not have them should not display a reverse snobbery which says: "Now, don't you think you are great!"

In the first chapter the need for greater imagination in listing the gifts was emphasized. Though it is not possible to type and name precisely all of the gifts, it may be helpful to look more closely at specific categories and common gifts. One common distinction has been between the gift of persons and gifts which come to persons. In Ephesians 4:11, 12, apostles, prophets, evangelists, pastors, and teachers are listed as gifts for the purpose of equipping the saints for the work of ministry and "for building up the body of Christ."

Our egalitarianism may make it difficult for us to recognize leaders as gifts. In any community, leaders emerge. Real problems often arise when a group in reality has leaders but pretends as if it does not. It is important to name the gifts in order to apply the communal test. When the gift of leadership is employed to serve instead of lording over others, then we can truly respond in thanksgiving for such a manifestation of grace. The Brethren once knew greater pluralism in leadership. Without eliminating pastors, some of us feel that we need to explore new ways to revive a kind of pluralism, which refuses to require one person to possess all the gifts. Such would represent more the Pauline model in which the variety of gifts is reflected in the pluralism of leadership.

The chapter on gifts, 1 Corinthians 12, closes with a lengthy list of leaders: "first apostles, second prophets, third teachers, then workers of miracles, then healers, helpers, administrators, speakers in various kinds of tongues." Perhaps Paul placed speakers in tongues last in order to preach humility to those at Corinth who may have been too puffed up. It can just as easily be asserted, however, that those who spoke in tongues were included to illustrate that God values a wide variety of gifts in the church. At Corinth Paul probably recognized the importance of leadership roles, such as apostles, prophets, and teachers, as a part of the process of testing charismatic threats to the community. The first reference to the conveying of the spirit by the laying on of hands occurred with the passing of the mantle of leadership from Moses to Joshua (Deut. 34:9). Ever since, the laying on of hands has been used to signify the Spirit's power as the group's authority is vested in one of its members.

From the many gifts, classical Pentecostalism has focused on the nine listed in 1 Corinthians 12:8-10. Since others have been discussed above and in the first chapter, here it may be helpful to be in dialogue with the ones which are more often featured. These nine may be grouped into three categories of three each, namely, the gifts to *say,* the gifts to *do,* and the gifts to *know.*[7]

The gifts *to say* are prophecy, tongues, and the interpretation of tongues:

Prophecy. Paul wanted the Corinthians to "earnestly desire the spiritual gifts" especially that of prophecy (1 Cor. 14:1). What was the nature of this gift which Paul seemed to prefer to some of the others (1 Cor. 11:5)? Prophecy was in direct line with the experience of Israel. It is not easy to be precise concerning the content of early Christian prophecy. It may have included predictions, proclamation of the kingdom coming, naming leaders, testimonies, and inspired edification. Though it was varied, there are four aspects which come through clearly. First, it was a direct word from God for the guidance of the community. The model which this suggests may be somewhat akin to traditional Quaker worship. Second, it knew the advantage of being clear speech, which did not need any interpretation. Third, its purpose was to speak words of upbuilding, encouragement, and consolation. Special revelations were to be tested by apostolic authority and teaching in light of this purpose.

Fourth, any one in the community could prophesy. This phenomenon prompts current scholars to suggest that the admonition to the women to keep silent (1 Cor. 14:35) refers in the Greek to the idle conversation or gossip which was disruptive to the order of congregational life, not to prophetic utterance.

Tongues. Since there has been a more extensive treatment of this gift in the first chapter, the discussion here will be limited to the context at Corinth. Paul valued *glossolalia* as an evidence of the Spirit speaking through believers. The gift of tongues was associated with prayer, praise, and thanksgiving. Primarily for the edification of the individual, the more spectacular *charismata* are totally a family affair. They are useless for missionary purposes. Guidelines on the use of tongues were necessary because of the disruption and dissension which they brought to the fellowship at Corinth.

Interpretation. Because of the controversy over tongues, Paul desired to regulate the gift carefully without forbidding it. Those who have this gift are urged to pray for the gift of interpretation (1 Cor. 14:13). It is difficult to know exactly what was involved. That it is interpretation, not translation, means sharing a leading from the Lord in a manner which can be understood by all. Tongues *plus* interpretation may have been equated with prophecy to some degree.

The gifts *to do* are healings, miracles, and faith:

Healing. Because of the popularity of the faith healing movement and the historic practice of anointing for healing among the Brethren, this is an area for real interchange and dialogue. Charismatics and Brethren affirm together the presence of healings in the New Testament church and the continuing healing work of the Spirit. The Brethren anointing service as appropriated from the fifth chapter of James needs to be compared with current phenomena. Though it is important for Brethren to be aware of the differences, the judgment which may fall on the popular movement only applies to some aspects and some parts of it. The activity is too varied to be able to place all faith healers under the same tent.

Some leaders of the current movement seem to reverse the frequent admonition of Jesus not to tell others. They tell everybody, often exploiting such healings for great personal financial gain. Brethren, on the other hand, are often too reluctant to

testify to gifts of healing. One of the tragedies, which serves likewise as a judgment, occurs when members travel far and seek
out popular faith healers when the anointing service is as near
and available as their telephone. Although it would be a mistake
to make too much out of the prooftexts about not telling others,
there is a value in a certain reticence and reverence in sharing
wondrous works of God.

Another basic difference concerns those few in the
charismatic movement who feel it is a lack of faith to utilize
medical means. The Brethren have emphasized that all healing
is God's work, whether through the laying on of hands and oil
or through hospitals and the skill of the physician. Neither have
we offered absolute promises of healing depending on the
degree of faith. This difference can be discerned in the threefold
action which is a part of the anointing service. The first anointing for the restoration of physical health indicates an openness
and an expectancy in terms of the healing and powerful work of
the Spirit. A second action for the forgiveness of sin calls for a
healing of relationships which can both transcend and influence
physical health. The third anointing of oil on the forehead is for
strengthening of faith, a faith which involves trust in God whatever lies ahead, a faith which does not attempt to manipulate
God but rather prays, "Thy will be done."

Miracles. Without denying the gift of working miracles in
healing and the supernatural, some of the manuscripts use here
the word for energy or power. In this reading we are dealing
with the effects of power. These gifts point to the special power
that God gives to some Christians to influence others by their
words and deeds.[8] In any event, miracles are not so much viola-
tions of the natural, as they are means of restoring creation as
God intended it to be.

Faith. It is generally agreed that faith here is not justifying
faith, by which one responds to the grace of God. Rather here is
a special faith so as to be able to remove mountains, or to be
able to keep on trusting and living against all odds. Here is the
gift which gives the courage to be in the atmosphere of apparent
hopelessness and death.

And the gifts *to know* are knowledge, wisdom, and discernment.

Knowledge. At Corinth, where many were influenced by

currents of Gnosticism, the very name of which suggests a quest for *gnosis* or knowledge, those so influenced claimed a special knowledge of salvation not available to others, thus assuming a rather elitist posture. This produced a most unhealthy divisiveness. Paul wished to stress that the knowledge given by the Spirit is that of doing God's will, holiness, and charity toward others.

Wisdom. As a teacher I like to point out that the gift of the utterance of wisdom is the first one in the list. But Paul is not speaking of a wisdom which we claim for ourselves. Rather he is speaking of the gift of a wisdom which makes foolish the wisdom of this world. The gift of wisdom then may be common sense illuminated by the Spirit in such a way as to have a good understanding of the purposes of God, the way of Christ, and the sacred writings.

Discernment. Here Paul refers to the gift of abilities to test whether a spirit is from God or not. The community applies the christological and communal tests as discussed. In Anabaptist circles discernment has taken on another very important function, that of naming the special gifts of brothers and sisters in the body. This may be one of the most important. In the church we are so often asked to do this or that or to serve in an office or teach a class. But how often do others sit with us to attempt to discern together our real gifts so that they might be used for the good of the body and for service in the kingdom. A greater openness to this gift might mean that we would let the church program be shaped by our gifts instead of fitting persons into offices and slots.

The Sin Against the Holy Spirit

Therefore I tell you, every sin and blasphemy will be forgiven men, but the blasphemy against the Spirit will not be forgiven. And whoever says a word against the Son of man will be forgiven; but whoever speaks against the Holy Spirit will not be forgiven, either in this age or in the age to come (Matt. 12:31-32).

In the context of the close kinship between the Spirit and the community of faith, we may risk an interpretation of a passage which has remained puzzling. The idea is not that God does not want to forgive. The biblical writers tell us that grace is basic to the nature of God. God's wrath is nothing other than the inevitable working out of the rejection of God's love. For God is longsuffering, patient, and has imaged freedom in each one of us. Therefore, as long as we remain within the community of the Spirit, there is a possibility for restored relationships with others and with God. Every sin can be forgiven. Whenever we remove ourselves from the possibilities of such relationships, however, there is no opportunity for forgiveness. The sin against the Holy Spirit is the sin of cutting ourselves off from the community of the Spirit.

Chapter 4

THE FIRST FRUITS OF THE SPIRIT

We know that the whole creation has been groaning in
travail together until now; and not only the creation,
but we ourselves, who have the first fruits of the Spirit,
groan inwardly as we wait for adoption as sons, the redemption
    of our bodies (Romans 8:22-23)

And in the last days it shall be, God declares,
that I will pour out my Spirit upon all flesh,
and your sons and your daughters shall prophesy,
and your old men shall dream dreams;
yes, and on my menservants and my maidservants in those days
I will pour out my Spirit, and they shall prophesy
           (Acts 2:17-18, from Joel 2:28-29)

Spirit and Mission

Biblical phrases introducing the chapters thus far have featured the close association of the Spirit with God's gift of life, the Spirit of Jesus Christ, and the community of faith. In the two texts cited for this chapter, we see how the Spirit's power is related to *mission*. The Spirit has a missionary function, commissioning and sending disciples and empowering them to become witnesses to God's saving love for all the world. If spirits are to be tested by the Spirit of him who lived for others and died on a cross, then the work of the Spirit is to enable *us* to be persons for others. If our gifts and tasks are tested by whether or not they build up the community, the community in the power of the Holy Spirit will measure itself by its service for the kingdom of God in the world. The promises about a special outpouring of the Spirit became real in a new beginning at Pentecost. We can participate in the same reality and name the Spirit, as does Paul, the first fruits, an earnest, a down payment, the foretaste of the redemption of ourselves and all creation.

The Domestication of the Spirit

In the course of a week's lecture series at Goshen College, I took a break to return home briefly in order to meet with one class at Bethany and visit my family. My arrival in the Chicago suburbs coincided providentially with the entrance of my wife, Lois, into the emergency room of our local hospital. After long minutes of anxiety and a chance meeting with a friend who had overheard a conversation, I discovered that she had slipped on the ice. It seemed that I showed up at the hospital just at the right time to share in the relief of pain as her dislocated shoulder slipped back into place.

As I was to return to Goshen the next morning to speak on Jesus and the Spirit, I wondered how this experience might relate to what I might say. I wanted to be open to praising the Lord not only for the continual gift of life but for special guidance. Yet, I thought of some of my brothers and sisters who had known more tragic experiences and had not been at the right place at the right time. I certainly did not want to impart the message that God plays favorites. We truly did receive the Spirit through God's healing powers and through the many people who expressed their love and concern and were willing to do so much. But did I want to feature what the Spirit had done for us so much that I might cause others to lose sight of the wholeness of the activity of the Holy Spirit? Basically, I was struggling with the issue of how to witness to my gratefulness for the presence of the Spirit without encouraging a "give me" style of religion. What I did share the next morning was something of my struggle over what and how I should share.

I still need help from sisters and brothers to truly discern the gifts of the Spirit in such situations. I do believe, however, that one of the issues we need to consider is the current tendency to domesticate the Spirit. After a lengthy discussion of the gifts of the Spirit, Paul calls for a more excellent way, a movement from "seeking one's own" to a higher way of love (1 Cor. 13). Throughout his letters to the church at Corinth, Paul wanted to show how the Spirit of Christ was different from the false freedom of self-indulgence. Much of current media religion is popular because of the promise that the Spirit will meet our every need and desire. The focus is on what Jesus will do for me instead of what we need to do in the service of Jesus Christ. The message seems to be: "Seek first physical health, peace of mind, and worldly success," instead of the teaching of our Lord: "Seek first his kingdom and his righteousness and all these things shall be yours as well" (Matt. 6:33).

This does not mean that we forsake all self-interest or self-respect. It does mean that blessings *and* sufferings are indeed byproducts of seeking first the Way. The admonition of Jesus serves as a judgment on much of our "religious" activity: "For whoever would save his life will lose it, and whoever loses his life for my sake will find it" (Matt. 16:25). To truly live in the Spirit is to give up manipulative desires to use others and God for my own ends. Through adoption, rebirth, sanctification, the Spirit can make each one of us a real and full person. Rather than being isolated, however, real personhood means being found in the common movement of the Spirit which is poured out for all.

One of the symptoms and contributing causes of the tendency to domesticate the Spirit has been the mistranslation of biblical pronouns. In popular religious circles and songs the plural biblical pronouns are most often laid aside. The preoccupation is with "my God" instead of "our God." The Bible, carefully read, may not proclaim that Jesus loves *me* as much as that Jesus loves *us.* When one scans a concordance, it is easy to find references describing Christ as Saviour of Israel or the world but not as "personal Saviour." The second person pronoun *you,* which in English represents both singular and plural, in the New Testament is most often found in the plural. My "pietistic" leaning values revival and gospel songs which express personal faith. I would be among the last to vote to eliminate all such songs from our life together. When we become infatuated with the *I, me, my,* and *mine* language, however, we pervert the very nature of the gospel message. Our roots are revealed to be more in the American enlightenment and American individualism than in biblical faith.

Each one of us, nevertheless, should know the assurance of personal acceptance. We are to be personally committed. Individualism, the centering of life around self, represents the denial of biblical faith. The emphasis on the integrity and worth of each person does not. It is as true that communal wholeness is impossible without personal wholeness as it is that personal wholeness is impossible without communal wholeness. Our personal relationship with Christ means a· personal relationship to Christ's saving love for the world. The Spirit's work in conversion is one of effecting a death to prideful self-centeredness and an aliveness to Christ's mission. The saving activity of the Spirit inspires and nurtures a personal commitment to building up the body of Christ and participating in signs and manifestations of his kingdom of righteousness and peace.

Commissioning by the Spirit

But you shall receive power when the Holy Spirit has come upon you; and you shall be my witnesses in Jerusalem and in all Judea and Samaria and to the end of the earth (Acts 1:8).

It is the Spirit who stamps the mark of mission on the church. In the gospels the characteristic feature of the resurrection appearances is that they are commissioning experiences. As in the case of the Apostle Paul, they became a powerful motivating force for evangelism. When the Gospels speak of having the Spirit, it is in connection to mission. The root word for apostle is "sent one." At Pentecost the Spirit universalizes mission. Again and again Luke relates acts of the mission to Gentiles as being initiated by the Holy Spirit. The word for witness appears thirty times in the Book of Acts. In the history of the church missionary enthusiasm has been one of the fruits of the revival of the doctrine of the Spirit, including the phenomenal growth of the Pentecostal movement in the twentieth century.

The baptism of our Lord offers the best paradigm or pattern for the commissioning nature of the Spirit. The presence of the Spirit as symbolized by the dove accompanied the water baptism by John. The voice of the Spirit commissioned Jesus not only for messianic Sonship but for suffering service. His public ministry stands in the sign of the Spirit. His baptism by water and by Spirit marked the end of his period of isolation and the beginning of ministry. It has been suggested that through his baptism in the muddy waters of Jordan, Jesus declared his solidarity with sinners and consciously accepted his mission of service.

The significance of the baptism of our Lord has too often been neglected in the teaching of the church. The conferring of the special charge on Jesus needs to be related to the call each Christian receives at the time of baptism. In his helpful discussion of baptism, Jürgen Moltmann reiterates the traditional Brethren position that "in a congregation of baptized believers, baptism and confirmation coincide." This is what we have maintained by the close association of water and Spirit baptism historically. But Moltmann also observes that in a believers' tradition, "ordination approaches baptism directly, as the conferring of a special charge."[1] As the baptism of Jesus was accompanied by the Spirit's commissioning, so baptism for believers involves an ordination for ministry. For the Brethren the laying on of hands following water baptism not only symbolizes the presence of the Spirit through relationship with the community of faith but commissioning by that community for the liberating ministry of Christ. Such ordination theology and its derivation from the baptism of Jesus can be seen in one of the passages from the *Apology* of Alexander Mack, Jr.:

> Just as the Chief High Priest pledged himself to the Father through His baptism to make the entire rebelling creation subject to Him, so all of His followers with their baptism have pledged themselves by oath to Him to assist Him in this important task. That is why Peter calls them a royal priesthood (1 Pet. 2:9).[2]

Although the reality of the need for cleansing, repentance, and new birth should not be eliminated from water baptism, the muddy waters of the Jordan and horse tanks and creeks often used by the Brethren should remind us of the act of identification with the sins and suffering of the world. Baptism involves both a call to nonconformity to fallen society and a commission to serve for the reconciliation and liberation of this very world. Baptism symbolizes both a cleansing and willingness to get our hands dirty.

The ordination for ministry of each believer at the time of baptism will not eliminate subsequent laying on of hands to acknowledge the calling of the Spirit for specific deeds and tasks. The general call to become a part of the Spirit's liberating activity will be supplemented by special calls for service in the life of the community and on behalf of the mission of the community. The Spirit's role was often indicated in the passing of the mantle of leadership in Israel. When the prophets spoke of the Spirit of the Lord "resting upon" someone, they were describing the type of special call which we call ordination.

We have noted that Paul approved of a variety of special gifts for the common good. Historically, the Brethren have prayed for the power of the Spirit in the ordination of special ministers, the calling of moderators for tenured office, and the sending of missionaries. There are some who feel that we should utilize this practice to commission an even greater variety of manifestations of the gifts of the Spirit.

It should also be noted that when the commissioning community calls someone, it does not want a person who is merely an echo of itself. Rather than listening to itself, the community is committed to listen to the voice of Christ. For this reason the Spirit commissions a person not just as a spokesperson for the fellowship but for discerning the mind of Christ. Contrary to a contemporary mood, the voice of the Holy Spirit must never become equated with the majorities in the nation or even in the church.

The Eschatological Nature of the Spirit

In him you also, who have heard the word of truth, the gospel of your salvation, and have believed in him, were sealed with the promised Holy Spirit, which is the guarantee (earnest) of our inheritance until we acquire possession of it, to the praise of his glory (Eph. 1:13-14).

We have indicated that the prophet Joel promised an out-pouring of the Spirit in the last days (the eschaton), when both the sons and daughters of the people of God will prophesy. Jesus promised his disciples that the Paraclete, the comforter, the advocate, the Spirit, would be with them after he was no longer present. The fullness of the Spirit was related to God's promises for the future. When Paul spoke of the present activity of the Spirit as being a guarantee or earnest, which means down payment or first installment, he was speaking of the now, not-yet, nature of the kingdom. Though we cannot know the precise time for the fulfillment of all of God's promises, we can begin to live those promises now. Though the kingdom of peace and righteousness has not yet come in its fulness, we can know a foretaste, the first fruits, of the kingdom now. The Spirit, who is the power of the kingdom, offers the first fruits of the harvest of the kingdom to the church for its agenda in mission.

The not-yet reality of the kingdom means that we can never identify the kingdom with our particular understanding of it or our patterns of mission. The not-yet, however, does not mean that we refuse to accept the earnest of the Spirit. For example, if the promise truly says that both our daughters and sons will prophesy, it is not enough to say that such will only happen when the kingdom comes in its fullness. Neither does this teaching support those who say that the way of loving enemies of the Sermon on the Mount is not for us but only for the day when Jesus comes to set up the kingdom. To receive the Spirit, which is the first installment of the age to come, will mean that our sons and daughters will begin to prophesy now, and that the way of the Sermon on the Mount can begin to grace our lives now.

The Brethren, whether they have always known it or not, have symbolized in a dramatic way this eschatological or end-time presence of the Spirit in our midst. When I was a boy sitting around the love feast tables, I puzzled over what the elders might be talking about in their references to the messianic banquet. They even spoke of that perfect meal when we would all rest our heads on Abraham's bosom. Currently, theologians are again writing about the messianic banquet or feast. Jesus himself compared the approaching kingdom of God with a marriage feast. It is the Spirit who gives a foretaste of the new creation in the feast. In terms of the common meal we eat together, this means that we do not yet know perfect love as we gather round the tables. We have experienced alienation; we know our differences. But we can experience a foretaste or the first fruits of that kind of fellowship which God desires for all and plans to give in the fullness of the kingdom. The same is true in the washing of one another's feet. We dare not pretend we perfectly serve. But we can participate in a beginning, a paradigm, of the style we hope to follow in our daily lives. This in turn is but a foretaste of God's gift of the Suffering Servant for all.

In the eschatological tension between the now and not-yet of the Spirit, there is no distinction between the individual and society. The earnest or down payment of the Spirit is the future good which has become present for the person of faith. It is also the power of the future kingdom of justice and peace breaking into the present. Many Mennonites are writing of the impossibility of separating the gospel of peace for the individual from the gospel of peacemaking on behalf of the kingdom. Evangelism and peacemaking belong together. In some charismatic circles the gospel for the person and the gospel for the kingdom have been separated in such a way as to suggest that a filling of the Spirit must precede a sending by the Spirit. Or it is preached that the good news of salvation is primary and discipleship is at best secondary. It is difficult to find any prioritizing in the New Testament. The gospel for the individual and the gospel of the kingdom is one gospel. To become new creatures in Christ is to begin simultaneously to become a part of a new creation, where the dividing walls of hostility are being broken down. Unlike most religious fervor today, the Spirit-filled revivals associated with Charles Finney refused to separate personal salvation from the social sphere. All the while stressing the necessity of personal sanctification, Finney argued at the same time that true revivalism involves taking the right stand in regards to questions about human rights. This was applied to the slavery issue, to women's rights, and to the area of peace. He declared that the Spirit of God is absent from any church which fails to speak out on such issues.[3] Whether one has an optimistic or very pessimistic analysis of our contemporary world, it is the Spirit who in joining the personal and social makes con-

crete the now, the beginnings, of the eschatological promises of
God.

Contemporary Applications

In response to my probing, some charismatics have explained why they do not share in activity which concerns racism, militarism and struggles for greater justice. They have related that their social action is to pray for their cities, the rulers, and for the peoples of the world. The power of prayer, they judge, can effect more concrete changes for good than all of the social action of the churches. They share in a valid critique of our attempt to roll up our sleeves and build the kingdom on earth apart from the Spirit's power. But they ignore both the commissioning and eschatological nature of the Spirit in feeling that the prayer for the Spirit's presence does not mean participation in the work of the Spirit.

Not all charismatics, however, ignore this larger calling. Many testify that their Spirit-baptism has led to greater involvement in corporate concerns than ever before. Unfortunately, many Brethren charismatics have felt that their experience means a discontinuity with the pacifism, style of service, and prophetic witness which was a part of the liberal social-gospel atmosphere of their youth. For many charismatics from other traditions, however, a break with their past has meant increased participation in kingdom concerns of freedom, peace, and righteousness.

The Roman Catholic charismatic movement especially seems to be characterized by voices who refuse to separate the gifts from the mission of the Spirit. From my many visits to Pentecostal and charismatic meetings, there is one which stands out for those of us who are attempting to exercise the gift of discernment. A few students and I attended a small Roman Catholic charismatic meeting of members from Chicago's south side. It was obvious that the twenty to twenty-five Christians sitting in a circle deeply cared for one another. The prayers, songs, tongues, testimonies all seemed genuine, orderly, and beautiful. The membership transcended the many divisions which so often divide Christians. There were blacks and whites, single and married, very poor and middle class, men and women, teen-agers and grandmothers. Aware of the rejoicing over two recent healings, we were somewhat surprised to discover that the references were to two marriages which had been saved by the work of the Spirit through the prayerful concern and deep interest of each member. Near the close of the meeting each person shared accountability in terms of their commitments to social action projects of one kind or another. In questioning a priest who was a member of the group, I discovered his biblical understandings seemed to avoid many of the errors analyzed in this book. In fact, his theology provided the basis for some of the assumptions which have permeated this study.

Rather than focusing exclusively on unlovely attitudes, disruption, and self-righteous manifestations, more of us need to model the "Spirit" movement at its best. Many charismatics have discovered the communal nature of the Spirit. Charismatic communities have emerged in contrast to the individualism of much of the movement. Communities such as the Church of the Redeemer in Houston, Texas, have provided models which signal hope for the possible reformation of the church. Charismatic leaders such as Graham Pulkingham can provide for Brethren, both within and outside the movement, a theology which joins the best from the charismatic experience with the best from our own communal teaching about the Spirit. Reba Place Fellowship in Evanston, Illinois, and the Sojourners community in Washington, D.C. have incorporated valid biblical ingredients from the charismatic movement into a more wholistic awareness of the work of the Spirit and the persons of the Trinity. Within charismatic circles, Sheila Macmanus Fahey has prepared a reflection and resource manual in the area of charismatic social action.[4]

The Spirit is working in similar ways in world Christianity. In answer to the altered situation in our world, there has been a growing realization that we all live in a missionary situation. The unilateral western mission, built on the assumption that some nations are Christian and others are not, is being replaced by multilateral world mission reflecting the Spirit movement's emphasis on renewal, prophecy, and power for the common people. The awareness of our need for greater unity, the universality of the kingdom of God, and the ministry of all believers, are themes which are surfacing in gatherings of Christians from all parts of the world. Following the lead of earlier Pentecostals the World Council of Churches has been discovering that reading the Bible through the eyes of the poor is a much different experience than through the eyes of most of us with full bellies. Pentecostals in the World Council of Churches are joining with their brothers and sisters in the assertion that the gifts of the Spirit need to be used not only for the edification of the church but for the good of the world. As the work of the Spirit becomes visible through baptism, the Lord's supper, special gifts, and ministries, the power of the Holy Spirit leads the church beyond itself out into the suffering of the world, enabling it to participate in the divine future of the presence of the kingdom of God.

Postscript:

BLESSED TRINITY

Blessed Trinity

Since we have affirmed the contemporary interest in the Spirit, while at the same time espousing the need to view the Spirit in relation to the other persons of the Trinity, a postscript may be helpful concerning the doctrine of the Trinity. The mystery of how one can be three and three can be one has provided the impetus for much theological and philosophical speculation. Nevertheless, the nature of the plurality of the Godhead has remained somewhat of a mystery throughout Christian history. In an attempt to clarify, Augustine employed threefold comparisons such as memory, understanding, will; lover, loved, love. Others have utilized personal analogies, such as the suggestion that one can be a mother, daughter, and sister at the same time one is a unique person. One of the most helpful ways of looking at the trinity for me has been a historical approach. The trinity was not dreamed up in a vacuum. Rather, it happened. The doctrine was not handed down in a neat logical package from the beginning. Since there was so much that had happened, the trinity developed as one of the ways to interpret what had happened.

Michael Green compares these happenings to a three-act drama.[1] Act One highlights the Jewish background of the first Christians. They were strict monotheists who believed in only one God, whose holiness was such that the name could not be pronounced and whose nature was too inscrutable to reproduce in any image. In Act Two, a man lived among them. After being with Jesus of Nazareth, listening to his teaching, and witnessing his character and manner of death, they were convinced that he brought God in focus. God's nature was unveiled through a person. But this was not another God. The God of Jesus, the Christ, they felt, was the same as the God of Abraham, Isaac, and Jacob. In Act Three we find the disciples discouraged and defeated following the crucifixion. Through the resurrection appearances and a powerful experience when they had come together, however, they were convinced that God's activity was still in their midst and that they were experiencing nothing less than the continued work and presence of Jesus among them.

The Trinity may be experienced by each one of us in similar ways. Gazing into the starry firmament or deeply aware of our finitude, we might know an awareness of something or Someone who is beyond our little systems, feeble efforts, and provincial lives. Or in moments of special encounters with the good, the beautiful, and the true, we may name glimpses of the ultimate as God. When we are met by persons, who are in the stream of persons tracing their history back to Jesus, we judge as divinely human the love and abundant life we receive. And in those moments when we are gifted with the fresh power of new perspectives, faith, gifts, and hope, we know the presence of the Holy Spirit. When we are tempted to be too chummy with God, we need the reminder that God is too big to ever get our arms completely around. When God is too removed, we can welcome the message of the Spirit's nearness. When God is inscrutable, it is good to know the glory of God in the face of One who walked and talked here on earth. When all of this seems to have been so long ago, it is enlivening to hear the message of the risen Christ. When we are tossed to and fro by so many spirits, we are blessed with the community to help us discern the Holy Spirit. As we encounter meaninglessness, brokenness, despair, and the powers and principalities, we can offer praise for the power and promise of the Spirit as first fruits of the kingdom of love.

NOTES
STUDY QUESTIONS

NOTES

Chapter 1: THE SPIRIT GIVES LIFE

[1] A somewhat fuller account can be found in Donald Durnbaugh's article, "Relationships of the Brethren with the Mennonites and Quakers, 1708-1865," *Church History* (March, 1966), pp. 9-10. For the purposes of our discussion, we are omitting any of the observer's references to Ephrata.

[2] See the balanced assessment of the topic in the statement of the Church of the Brethren General Board, *The Holy Spirit, the Church, and the Charismatic Movement* (adopted by Annual Conference Standing Committee, June, 1977, available on request).

[3] Michael Green, *I Believe in the Holy Spirit* (Grand Rapids: Eerdmans, 1976), p. 209.

[4] Walter Hollenweger, "'Touching' and 'Thinking' the Spirit: Some Aspects of European Charismatics," in a book edited by Russell Spittler, *Perspectives on the New Pentecostalism* (Grand Rapids: Baker, 1976), p. 65.

[5] James D. Dunn, *Jesus and the Spirit* (Philadelphia: Westminster, 1975), p. 149.

[6] Richard Baer, Jr., "Quaker Silence, Catholic Liturgy, and Pentecostal Glossolalia," in *Perspectives on the New Pentecostalism,* pp. 150-64.

[7] Green, *op. cit.,* p. 198.

[8] Clark Pinnock, "The New Pentecostalism: Reflections of an Evangelical Observer," *Perspectives on the New Pentecostalism,* p. 190.

Chapter 2: THE LORD IS THE SPIRIT

[1] *Ruach* (Spirit) in Hebrew is feminine, and in the coming of God through creation and a Person the Spirit broods like a mother dove. Combine this with the masculine activity of the Spirit in the conception of Jesus and one may have a justification for employing either "her" or "his" as personal pronouns for the Spirit. At the same time we proclaim there is neither male or female in the Holy Spirit. God transcends the distinction of sex, representing beforehand and on a higher level whatever is of value in sexuality.

[2] John Macquarrie, *Principles of Christian Theology* (New York: Charles Scribner's Sons, 1977), pages 330-32.

[3] From H. T. Kerr, *A Compend of Luther's Theology* (Philadelphia: The Westminster Press, 1943), p. 57.

[4] Donald Durnbaugh, editor, *European Origins of the Brethren* (Elgin: Brethren Press, 1958), p. 386

Chapter 3: THE FELLOWSHIP OF THE HOLY SPIRIT

[1] J. Massyngberde Ford, "The New Pentecostalism: Personal

Reflections of a Participating Roman Catholic Scholar," *Perspectives on the New Pentecostalism,* p. 214.

[2] For a good discussion and documentation of these points see Michael Green, *I Believe in the Holy Spirit,* pp. 139-47.

[3] Donald Durnbaugh, editor, *The Brethren in Colonial America* (Elgin: The Brethren Press, 1967), pp. 445-46.

[4] Alexander Mack, Jr. in his "Apologia," as found in Donald Durnbaugh, *The Brethren in Colonial America* (Elgin: The Brethren Press, 1967), p. 503.

[5] George Montague, *The Holy Spirit: Growth of a Biblical Tradition* (New York: Paulist Press, 1976), pp. 277-83.

[6] See John Kildahl, *The Psychology of Speaking in Tongues* (New York: Harper and Row, 1972).

[7] Michael Green, *I Believe in the Holy Spirit,* p. 161. Excellent analyses of each of the nine follows his initial suggested clarification.

[8] *Ibid.,* pp. 177-80.

Chapter 4: THE FIRST FRUITS OF THE SPIRIT

[1] Jurgen Moltmann, *The Church in the Power of the Spirit* (New York: Harper & Row, 1977), p. 314.

[2] Alexander Mack, Jr. *"Apologia,"* op. cit., p. 510.

[3] Donald Dayton, *Discovering an Evangelical Heritage* (New York: Harper & Row, 1976), pp. 17-19. See the entire book for an excellent analysis of a revivalism and evangelism which was wedded to the gospel of peace.

[4] Sheila Macmanus Fahey, *Charismatic Social Action* (New York: Paulist Press, 1977). A good practical guide for charismatics in many areas of social witness such as drugs, penal system, the aged, hunger, race, poverty, mental illness, etc.

Postscript: BLESSED TRINITY

[1] Michael Green, *I Believe in the Holy Spirit,* pp. 14-17.

STUDY QUESTIONS

Chapter 1: THE SPIRIT GIVES LIFE

1. The chapter titles are lifted from biblical passages about the Holy Spirit. If you were giving biblical definitions of the Holy Spirit, what are some you might add to the four found in the table of contents?

2. What New Testament Greek words cited by the author underlie the word *charismatic?* In what sense can all Christians claim to be charismatic?

3. The early critic of the Pennsylvania sects writes of the "great clamor" in his caricature of early Brethren worship. Are you disturbed or pleased that the early Brethren may have been somewhat more noisy than the Quakers or Mennonites? How would you relate and priorize the place of reason and emotion in worship?

4. Do you agree with the mood of the Spirit-movement, which feels that we should live in a much greater degree of expectancy concerning contemporary manifestations of the Holy Spirit? Why or why not?

5. Krister Stendahl proposes a greater use of our imaginations in thinking of the gifts of the Spirit. He mentions the gift of words when we are called before magistrates because we have gotten in trouble because of our faith. He also mentions special gifts in relation to administration. Can you think of others which are neglected or not often mentioned?

6. Should the church encourage or discourage the manifestation of the gift of tongues? Give arguments from your own experience and/or reflect on those of the author.

Chapter 2: THE LORD IS THE SPIRIT

1. This chapter concerns testing the spirits. Concretely, how do we work at the matter of testing whether a divine leading is of the Holy Spirit or a human spirit? In what ways does Jesus become the test?

2. Read or reread Luther's (somewhat humorous) reaction to his own vision. Do you agree with the basic point he was attempting to make?

3. Consider the debate in church history between East and West on whom the Spirit proceeds from. Can you see how the *filioque* clause might make a difference in Christian life?

4. What does the author mean when he contrasts a theology of glory with a theology of the cross? In what ways, if any, do you think the current spirit-movement neglects a theology of the cross?

5. How should one relate to a brother or sister who testifies to a miraculous healing when you discern that he or she may be dying?

6. Have you been close to situations like that described in reference to the advice given to William Beahm? How can we proclaim the promises of the gifts of the Spirit without seeming to judge the measure of faith of another?

Chapter 3: THE FELLOWSHIP OF THE SPIRIT

1. The author makes a strong case for Spirit and church belonging together. What New Testament passages support this connection?

2. How are Spirit-baptism and water baptism related in Brethren practice? Draw on data the author cites, as well as your own experience. Be sure to consider the practice of laying on hands.

3. Invite someone who testifies to the second baptism of the Holy Spirit to share the meaning of their experience with you or your class. At what points can you relate to their experience?

4. Can you view leaders as gifts of the Spirit as discussed in this chapter in connection with Ephesians 4? What categories of "leader-gifts" are represented in your congregation?

5. The fundamental Pauline test of the spirits is the communitarian test: Does the gift build up and edify the community? Does it serve the common good? But does this allow a person to stand over against the community in a prophetic role? If so, how?

6. What are some contemporary equivalents of the nine gifts listed in 1 Corinthians 12?

Chapter 4: THE FIRST FRUITS OF THE SPIRIT

1. What are the "first fruits" or "earnest" of the Spirit of which the author speaks? What does it mean to live in the tension between the now and the not-yet?

2. In what way does the Love Feast allow us to experiment a foretaste of the kingdom, of the end-time presence of the Spirit?

3. What does the author mean when he speaks of the domestication of the Spirit? Do you agree that popular religion focuses more on what Jesus does for me instead of how we should respond to Jesus? Do you agree with popular religion?

4. How and when does the Spirit commission us to act and to serve? Do you agree with the idea that baptism is an ordination to ministry? Why or why not?

5. As Quakers, Mennonites, and Brethren have come together for a New Call to Peacemaking, many are arguing that evangelism and peacemaking belong together. Do you agree? Why or why not?

6. The author feels that instead of either rejecting or accepting uncritically the current charismatic movement, we need to model it at its best. Do you agree? What are some examples of the movement at its best?